Terminology in the 21st Century: Many Faces, Many Places (Term21)

Held at LREC 2022

Marseille, France
20 – 25 June 2022

Editors:

Rute Costa
Sara Carvalho
Ana Ostroski Anic
Anas Fahad Khan

ISBN: 978-1-7138-6142-3

Printed from e-media with permission by:

Curran Associates, Inc.
57 Morehouse Lane
Red Hook, NY 12571

CURRAN ASSOCIATES INC.
proceedings
.com

Some format issues inherent in the e-media version may also appear in this print version.

Association for Computational Linguistics
209 N. Eighth Street
Stroudsburg, Pennsylvania 18360

Phone: 1-570-476-8006
Fax: 1-570-476-0860

acl@aclweb.org

Additional copies of this publication are available from:

Curran Associates, Inc.
57 Morehouse Lane
Red Hook, NY 12571 USA
Phone: 845-758-0400
Fax: 845-758-2633
Email: curran@proceedings.com
Web: www.proceedings.com

LREC 2022 Workshop
Language Resources and Evaluation Conference
20-25 June 2022

**Terminology in the 21st century:
many faces, many places
(Term21)**

PROCEEDINGS

Editors:
Rute Costa
Sara Carvalho
Ana Ostroški Anić
Anas Fahad Khan

Proceedings of the LREC 2022 Workshop on Terminology in the 21st century: many faces, many places (Term21)

Edited by:
Rute Costa, Sara Carvalho, Ana Ostroški Anić, Anas Fahad Khan

For more information:
European Language Resources Association (ELRA)
9 rue des Cordelières
75013, Paris
France
http://www.elra.info
Email: lrec@elda.org

Preface

The Term21 (Terminology in the 21st century: many faces, many places) workshop aims to provide a discussion forum regarding the theoretical and methodological approaches that have characterised Terminology in recent years. In particular, it focuses on the connection to the Linguistic Linked (Open) Data paradigm and to Semantic Web technologies through the use of ontologies, as well as on how these approaches promote the creation of interoperable terminological resources in multiple domains and applications, such as Digital Humanities, elexicography, or eHealth. In addition, this workshop addresses current Terminology-related standards and their inherent advantages and challenges.

Following previous initiatives at LREC set up by members of the organising and programme committees (Lisbon, 2004, Genova, 2006, and Portoroz, 2016), Term21 is taking place within the framework of the NexusLinguarum COST Action – European network for Web-centred linguistic data science (CA 18209) and of the MORDigital project – Digitalização do Diccionario da Lingua Portugueza de António de Morais Silva [PTDC/LLTLIN/6841/2020]. Term21's first edition is held in conjunction with LREC 2022 in Marseille, France, on June 20, 2022.

The workshop accepted eight papers, seven of which have been included in this volume. Four of the papers focus on Automatic Term Extraction (ATE), one on a lexicon-driven approach to Terminology, one on how knowledge organisation can contribute to language simplification, and one on the conversion to the TBX format.

As regards the topic of ATE, the paper by Banerjee et al., entitled *A Dataset for Term Extraction in Hindi*, introduces the first term-annotated dataset for Hindi, based on texts in the field of education, while also addressing the underlying challenges of annotation for under-resourced languages. Nazar and Lindemann, in the paper *Terminology extraction using co-occurrence patters as predictors of semantic relevance*, propose a method for ATE in which term co-occurrence is used as a statistical measure, contributing to ranking term candidates according to their semantic relevance to a specific domain. This method is applied to a Spanish-English Linguistics corpus. In the paper *Evaluating Pre-Trained Language Models for Focused Terminology Extraction from Swedish Medical Records*, Jerdhaf et al. compare the performance of a generalist Swedish pre-trained language model with a domain-specific Swedish pre-trained model focusing on implant terms. The fourth paper related to ATE is authored by Rigouts Terryn et al. and is entitled *D-Terminer; Online Demo for Monolingual and Bilingual Automatic Term Extraction*. The paper presents an open access, online demo for monolingual and multilingual ATE from parallel corpora, as well as the updated version (1.5) of the Annotated Corpora for Term Extraction Research (ACTER) dataset.

In the paper *Lexicon-driven approach for Terminology: specialized resources on the environment in Brazilian Portuguese*, and following a lexicon-driven approach to terminology work, Arraes describes ongoing collaboration, especially in what concerns content in Brazilian Portuguese, for the development of DiCoEnviro (Dictionnaire Fondamental de Environnement – Fundamental Dictionary on the environment), a multilingual terminological resource developed by the Observatoire de Linguistique Sens Texte at the University of Montreal, Canada. The paper *Knowledge Representation and Language Simplification of Human Rights*, by Silecchia et al., addresses a very recent interdisciplinary project aiming at analysing both the conceptual and linguistic dimensions of human rights terminology, with the goal of developing a new knowledge-based multilingual terminological resource designed to meet the FAIR principles for Open Science. In the future, the authors intend to develop a prototype for the simplified rewriting of international legal texts relating to human rights, in order to facilitate their comprehension by non-experts.

Finally, in the paper *Converting from the Nordic Terminological Record Format to the TBX Format*, Skeppstedt et al. describe work carried out by the Institute for Language and Folklore within the Federated eTranslation TermBank Network Action and focus on the challenges of converting from the Nordic Terminological Record Format, as used in Rikstermbanken (Sweden's National Term Bank), to the TermBase eXchange (TBX) format.

Overall, these contributions address several of the current research topics in Terminology, namely the challenges underlying the role of Natural Language Processing in the automation of terminology-related tasks, the connection between the linguistic and the conceptual dimensions of terminology work, as well as data formats and interoperability. The diversity of domains explored in the papers (e.g. humanities and social sciences, medicine, law, the environment) also illustrates that, indeed, Terminology is increasingly developing in the confluence of many "faces" and "places".

We would like to thank the programme committee for their careful and constructive reviews, which have contributed to the quality of the event. We also would like to acknowledge the support from the MORDigital – Digitalização do Diccionario da Lingua Portugueza de António de Morais Silva [PTDC/LLT-LIN/6841/2020] project, financed by the Portuguese National Funding through the FCT – Fundação para a Ciência e Tecnologia.

Rute Costa
Sara Carvalho
Ana Ostroški Anić
Anas Fahad Khan

Organizers

Rute Costa - NOVA FCSH/NOVA CLUNL
Sara Carvalho - Universidade de Aveiro/NOVA CLUNL
Ana Ostroški Anić - Institute for Croatian Language and Linguistics
Anas Fahad Khan - Istituto di Linguistica Computazionale

Program Committee

Ana Ostroški Anić, Institute for Croatian Language and Linguistics (CROATIA)
Anas Fahad Khan, Istituto di Linguistica Computazionale (ITALY)
Bruno Almeida, ROSSIO Infrastructure / NOVA CLUNL (PORTUGAL)
Christian Chiarcos, Goethe University Frankfurt (GERMANY)
Federica Vezzani, Università di Padova (ITALY)
Giorgio Di Nunzio, Università di Padova (ITALY)
Laurent Romary, INRIA (FRANCE)
Maria José Bocorny Finatto, Universidade Federal do Rio Grande do Sul (BRAZIL)
Melania Cabezas García, University of Granada (SPAIN)
Pamela Faber, University of Granada (SPAIN)
Patrick Drouin, Montreal University (CANADA)
Penny Labropoulou, Institute of Language and Speech (GREECE)
Rute Costa, NOVA FCSH / NOVA CLUNL (PORTUGAL)
Sara Carvalho, Universidade de Aveiro / NOVA CLUNL (PORTUGAL)
Silvia Piccini, Istituto di Linguistica Computazionale (ITALY)
Sue Ellen Wright, Kent State University (USA)
Sylvie Desprès, Université Paris 13 (FRANCE)
Thierry Declerck, DFKI GmbH (GERMANY)
Ulrich Heid, University of Hildesheim (GERMANY)

Table of Contents

Workshop Program

Monday, June 20, 2022

14:00–14:10 ***Opening session***

14:10–14:35 *Linking general and specialized semantic frames in AirFrame*
Ana Ostroški Anić

14:35–15:00 *Lexicon-driven approach for Terminology: specialized resources on the environment in Brazilian Portuguese*
Flávia Lamberti Arraes

15:00–15:25 *Knowledge Representation and Language Simplification of Human Rights*
Sara Silecchia, Federica Vezzani and Giorgio Maria Di Nunzio

15:25–15:50 *Converting from the Nordic Terminological Record Format to the TBX Format*
Maria Skeppstedt, Marie Mattson, Magnus Ahltorp and Rickard Domeij

15:50–16:20 ***Coffee break***

16:20–16:45 *A Dataset for Term Extraction in Hindi*
Shubhanker Banerjee, Bharathi Raja Chakravarthi and John Philip McCrae

16:45–17:10 *Terminology extraction using co-occurrence patterns as predictors of semantic relevance*
Rogelio Nazar and David Lindemann

17:10–17:35 *Evaluating Pre-Trained Language Models for Focused Terminology Extraction from Swedish Medical Records*
Oskar Jerdhaf, Marina Santini, Peter Lundberg, Tomas Bjerner, Yosef Al-Abasse, Arne Jonsson and Thomas Vakili

17:35–18:00 *D-Terminer: Online Demo for Monolingual and Bilingual Automatic Term Extraction*
Ayla Rigouts Terryn, Veronique Hoste and Els Lefever

18:00–18:10 ***Discussion + Closing session***

Proceedings of the TERM21 Workshop , pages 1–7
Language Resources and Evaluation Conference (LREC 2022), Marseille, 20-25 June 2022

Lexicon-driven Approach for Terminology: specialized resources on the environment in Brazilian Portuguese

Flávia Lamberti Arraes
Departamento de Línguas Estrangeiras e Tradução
Instituto de Letras, Universidade de Brasília, ICC – Ala Sul –
Sala B1 167/63 - Campus Universitário Darcy Ribeiro – Asa Norte –
Brasília/DF CEP: 70910-900, Brazil
flavialamberti@unb.br, flavialamberti@gmail.com

Abstract

This paper presents a terminological research carried out to account for terms of the environment in Brazilian Portuguese based on a lexico-semantic perspective for Terminology (L'Homme, 2015, 2016, 2017, 2020; L'Homme et al., 2014, 2020). This work takes place in the context of a collaboration for the development of *DiCoEnviro* (*Dictionnaire Fondamental de l'Environnment* – Fundamental Dictionary on the environment), a multilingual terminological resource developed by the *Observatoire de Linguistique Sens Texte* at the *University of Montreal*, Canada. By following a methodolgy especially devised to develop terminological work based on a lexicon-driven approach (L'Homme et al., 2020), the terminological analysis reveals how the linguistic behavior of terms may be unveiled and how this is effective for identifying the meaning of a term and supporting meaning distinctions.

Keywords: Lexicon-driven approach, Terminology, Explanatory Combinatorial Lexicology, Frame Semantics, Environment

1. Introduction

This paper presents a terminological research carried out to account for terms of the environment in Brazilian Portuguese based on a lexico-semantic perspective for Terminology (L'Homme, 2015, 2016, 2017, 2020; L'Homme et al., 2014, 2020). This work takes place in the context of a collaboration for the development of *DiCoEnviro* (*Dictionnaire Fondamental de l'Environnment* – Fundamental Dictionary on the environment), a multilingual terminological resource developed by the *Observatoire de Linguistique Sens Texte* at the University of Montreal, Canada.

The perspective taken is innovative when compared to other specialized resources on the environment in Brazilian Portuguese. Existing resources on the environment (e.g. *Glossário do Meio Ambiente*, 2022) usually present lists of terms and multiword terms that show no relation between terms. It also includes compositional expressions (i.e. the whole meaning of the expression corresponds to the sum of its parts) that would have not been included as a whole had a lexicon-driven approach (LDA), for instance, been adopted in the analysis. An expression, such as *conservação ambiental*, is analyzed based on the relations each lexical unit establishes between themselves.

Taking a linguistic perspective to carry out terminological research, the LDA accounts not only for nouns, but also verbs, adjectives and adverbs. It also suggests criteria to identify terms and to support meaning distinctions by capturing the linguistic properties of terms, i.e. their predicative structure and lexical relations they establish between themselves. This is an effective approach to unveil the specialized knowledge of a domain. This knowledge is uncovered from running texts and is not based on predefined delimitations of concepts. By applying this approach, DiCoEnviro presents an expression of the domain of the environment through a web of relations in six languages, i.e. French, English, Spanish, Portuguese, Italian and more recently Chinese.

This paper shows how two specific lexical semantics frameworks can be applied to terms and help us to describe their linguistic properties: Explanatory Combinatorial Lexicology (Mel'čuk et al., 1995) and Frame Semantics, and its application in the FrameNet Project (Fillmore, 1982; Fillmore et al., 2003; Fillmore and Baker, 2010) (Section 2). In Section 3 we present the methodology used for the development of DiCoEnviro, with special reference to the corpus, term extraction and criteria to identify terms that refer to the Brazilian Portuguese version. In Section 4, we present a specific case analysis of a polysemious lexical item, *ambiental,* that led to meaning distinctions based on the shared relations between terms. We conclude by providing some figures regarding the work we have done up to now and mention some directions we wish to take in the future.

2. Theoretical frameworks

The lexicon-driven approach is of special assistance to terminological work as its focus is placed on the analysis of linguistic units, more specifically lexical units, as opposed to concepts as abstract generalizations of items of knowledge (L'Homme, 2020: 27). As a consequence, the approach is semasiological: it consists in delimiting lexical units that convey specialized meaning, often called terms, in running texts. The approach is 'relational': it consists in delimiting meaning of lexical units based on the relations they share with other units (L'Homme, 2020: 26). This last aspect is also especially important to support meaning distinctions. For instance, consider the lexical item *terra* in the following sentences:

Mas, enquanto a TERRA *é uma unidade formada por ecossistemas altamente integrados, o Mundo se apresenta, ao contrário, como uma realidade composta de sistemas culturais, sociais, políticos e naturais*, (...)
Atualmente existem estimativas com base em 6 categorias de uso da TERRA: *terra degradada ou consumida (por exemplo, aquela sob áreas construídas), terra sob jardins, terra agrícola.*

In the first sentence, the meaning of TERRA can be connected to that of other terms, such as *planeta* (planet), a generic term, *mundo* (world), a related meaning, and *sol* (sun) a constrastive one, whereas, in the second sentence, TERRA can be linked to *solo* (soil), a meronym, and to combinations such as ~ *degradada*, ~ *consumida*, ~ *agrícola*. This evidence tells us that we are dealing with two diferent meanings. DiCoEnviro presents two different entries to account for these two meanings: $Terra_1$ and $terra_2$.

The terminological analysis will examine different types of relations expressed via a number of what is called linguistic properties of terms. DiCoEnviro applies two specific lexical semantics frameworks that are especially equipped to capture the linguistic properties of the predicative terms: Explanatory Combinatorial Lexicology - ECL (Mel'čuk et al. 1995) and Frame Semantics, together with its application *FrameNet Project* (Fillmore, 1982; Fillmore et al., 2003; Fillmore and Baker, 2010)[1].

The linguistic properties of terms are captured by i) delimiting lexical meaning, i.e. determine if we are dealing with terms that are non-predicative, predicative or a quasi-predicative ones, as defined in Polguère (2016: 162), and ii) identifying lexical relations established between terms (paradigmatic and syntagmatic relations). Non-predicative terms does not require participants for the expression of their meaning; examples are terms such as Earth, water, air, planet, plant, tree, etc. Predicative terms, on the other hand, are expressed generally by verbs, nouns, adjectives, adverbs; their essential feature is that they require participants for the expression of their meaning. Predicative units require actants or arguments and can combine with optional participants (i.e. circumstantials). Obligatory participants (arguments) are stated in a structure called argument structure. DiCoEnviro presents the argument structure of predicative terms in each entry: e.g. a predicate term with two arguments, X and Y, in *absorver*: X (e.g. árvore) absorve Y (e.g. gás). Quasi-predicative terms share similarities with predicative units because they also require participants. Following we show the example of $terra_2$ in DiCoEnviro:
$terra_2$
uma terra: ~ utilizada por X (e.g. pelo homem) para atuar em Y (e.g. $plantação_2$).

Based on ECL (Mel'čuk et al. 1995: 125-152), DiCoEnviro also provides details on the types of lexical relations terms establish with other terms: i) paradigmatic relations are semantic relations that connect lexical units, such as terms that are semantically related or are opposites. For instance, the verbs $emitir_1$ and $liberar_1$ are semantically related, but $absorver_1$, and $emitir_1$, on the other hand, are opposite meanings, and ii) syntagmatic relations (most preferred combinations with other lexical units), such as syntagmatic relations that express a property of $terra_4$ (e.g. *terra agrícola, terra consumida, terra degradada*) and also combinations, e.g. *preparar a ~, cultivar a ~, manejar a ~*. Lexical relations are represented with a system called lexical functions (LFs) (Mel'čuk et al. 1995: 125-152).[2]

Frame Semantics (Fillmore, 1982; Fillmore and Baker, 2010) aims to establish a connection between language and abstract background knowledge. This connection is developed based on a methodology devised for the FrameNet projet (Fillmore et al. 2003; Ruppenhofer et al. 2016). This methodology has been applied, with adaptations, to develop specialized resources (L'Homme, 2015, 2016 ; L'Homme et al., 2020)[3].

As stated by L'Homme (2020: 45):

> In Frame Semantics, this background knowledge is structured in the form of ***semantic frames***. More precisely, a frame can be defined as the schematic modeling of a prototypical ***situation*** that includes ***participants***, which constitute its ***frame elements*** (***FEs***).

Furthermore, L'Homme (2020: 45) adds:

> In Frame Semantics, the meanings of LUs are understood, analyzed and described according to background knowledge captured in semantic frames : LUs are said to 'evoke' a frame.

By applying the methodology proposed in FrameNet and adapted for the development of specialized resources (L'Homme et al. 2020), the meaning of a term is described via annotation of contexts, which is a step within the terminological work methodology presented in the next section.

3. Methodology

The methodology applied to the Portuguese data follows the steps that are applied to other languages. It is bottom-up: in other words, terminological work starts from running texts based on which all the analysis is carried out. It comprises 8 steps, as outlined in L'Homme et al. (2020):

Compiling terminological entries:

[1] See L'Homme (2020: 39-50) for a detailed explanation.
[2] See L'Homme (2020), chapter 8.

[3] In Portuguese Frame semantics has been applied, for example, to the fields of football (Dicionário da Copa do Mundo 2014) and to Law (Pimentel 2013). See also FrameNet Brazil.

1. Compilation of specialized corpora
2. Identification of terms (semi-automated)
3. Selection and extraction of contexts
4. Definition of the argument structure
5. Annotation of contexts
Finding frames among lexical entries:
6. Definition of semantic frames
7. Encoding of frames
8. Definition of relations between frames
(L'Homme, Robichaud and Subirat, 2020)

The Brazilian Portuguese specialized corpus, on the subdomain of deforestation, has been compiled by Botta (2013) and is composed of scientific and journalistic texts published between 1981 and 2012. It contains approximately 277,000 words. Texts are queried with in Intercorpus[4], an online concordancer, which help us analyze and extract contexts.

A term extraction software, TermoStat (Drouin, 2003), is applied to the corpus and generates a list of candidate terms. The list is further analyzed manually to select terms based on criteria devised by L'Homme (2004: 64-66). For instance, *floresta*, *desmatamento*, *espécie*, *mata*, *vegetação*, *sustentabilidade*, are all selected based on the fact that these lexical units are related to the specialized domain. Other criteria are applied when the link with the specialized domain is not easily or clearly established. For instance, verbs and activity nouns (e.g. *manejar*$_1$, *manejo*$_1$) and adjectives (e.g. *ambiental*$_1$) require the application of a second criteria: the analysis of the nature of the semantic arguments that interact linguistically with the lexical unit in focus. If the arguments are terms validated by the first criterion (i.e. they are related to a specialized domain), the lexical unit in focus is also a term. For example, the verb *manejar*$_1$ requires two arguments: 1. someone (e.g. *homem*, *produtor*) that *maneja*; 2. the thing that is *manejado* (e.g. *floresta*, *mata*, *vegetação*). If arguments are validated as terms by the first criterion, the predicative unit is also considered a term. *Manejar* is considered a term because *homem*, *produtor*, *floresta*, *mata*, *vegetação* are regarded as terms. Other criteria are i) a morphological relationship with a term; for example, the adjective *manejado*$_1$ (e.g. *floresta ~*; *mata ~*; *vegetação ~*), is morphologically and semantically related to the verb and noun (*manejar*$_1$ and *manejo*$_1$); and ii) a paradigmatic relationship with the term. For example the term *ambiental*$_1$ holds a semantic relationship of quasi-synonym with *ecológico*$_1$ and a related meaning relation with *ambiental*$_2$.

Up to 20 contexts are then selected and extracted from the corpus and registered in a XML file in a database powered by Oxygen XML Editor. In this file, the argument structure is defined for predicative and quasi-predicative terms. Arguments are labeled with semantic roles. For instance, the arguments of *manejar* are: Agent *maneja* Patient; then a typical term, a recurrent term that instantiates the argument, is indicated: homem *maneja* floresta.

Based on the methodology developed within the FrameNet project, contexts are then annotated to specify semantic roles and syntactical functions. Below we present a sample of the annotated contexts for the term *manejar*.

O *setor* florestal brasileiro$_{[Agent]}$ vem adotando este conceito, **MANEJANDO** as ***florestas***$_{[Patient]}$ **com práticas e técnicas que visam o equilíbrio entre o desenvolvimento econômico e a manutenção dos recursos naturais.**$_{[Means]}$ [XYZ FatoseNumerosdoBrasilFlorestal_sbs 0 MGB 11/04/2013]

Uma *empresa* que produzisse lâminas faqueadas e desenroladas deveria **MANEJAR** sua ***floresta***$_{[Patient]}$ para produzir madeira de densidades média a leve. [XYZ MANEJOFLORESTAL_1996 0 MGB 11/04/2013]

A summary table is established after the annotations are finished presenting all the semantic roles and syntactical functions identified in the contexts.

MANEJAR 1		
Actantes		
Paciente	Objeto (SN) (10) Sujeito (SN) (4) Relação_indireta (Pro) Relação_indireta (SN) Sujeito (Pro)	floresta (8) vegetação (2) amazônia área este{uma vegetação já consolidada} gado pastagem qual sistema
Agente	Relação_indireta (Prop) Relação_indireta (SN) Relação_indireta (SV) Sujeito (SN)	empresa produtor quem setor

Figure 1: Summary table of the annotated contexts for *manejar*$_1$.

The last 3 steps of methodology (i.e. definition of frames; encoding of frames and definitions of relations between terms) are dedicated to connect the linguistic properties described to a conceptual background. As an example, we focus on the *Judgement_of_impact_on_the_environment* frame[5], which is evoked by terms in English (e.g. *clean*$_1$, *environmental*$_2$, *green*$_1$) French (e.g. *écologique*$_2$, *environnemental*$_2$, *proper*$_1$, *vert*$_1$) and Portuguese (e.g. *ambiental*$_2$, *ecológico*$_2$). This frame was defined based on i) the same number of arguments: all the terms have one argument; and ii) the nature of their semantic role: the arguments are labelled as Instrument, Cause and/or Means, and are instantiated by terms that denote an instrument, a

[4] Chièze, E.; Polguère, A. (no date) available at <http://olst.ling.umontreal.ca/intercorpus/>.

[5] See L'Homme et al. (2014) and L'Homme (2015) for more details on discovering frames in specialized domains.

cause and/or means: Instrument: en. *car*, *vehicle*, etc; fr. *voiture*, etc; Cause: en. *action, activity, conservation*, etc; fr. *action, étiquetage, protection*, etc; pt. *consciência, educação, gestão*, etc; Means: fr. *papier, contenant*, etc).

Based on the annotated contexts, it is possible to establish that the terms evoke the same situation (*Judgement_of_impact_on_the_environment*) whereby an instrument, a cause and/or means 'is designed to have minimum impact on the environment'[6]. Figure 2 below shows how this frame appears in the interface named *Framed DiCoEnviro*[7].

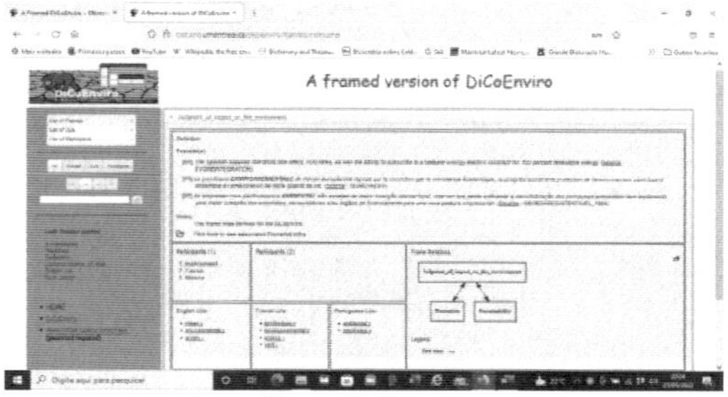

Figure 2. Frame *Judgement_of_impact_on_the_environment* in the Framed Version of DiCoEnviro.

Based on L'Homme et al. (2020), the encoding of the frame accounts for the following:

i) the name of the frame: for example, Judgement_of_impact_on_the_environment;
ii) a definition formulated for the field of the environment stating the obligatory participants: this has not been done yet for the frame in i);
iii) example(s) for each of the languages described:

EN] *The Spanish supplier Iberdrola now offers TOU rates, as well the ability to subscribe to a **GREEN** energy electric contract for 100 percent renewable energy.* (Source : EVGRIDINTEGRATION)

[FR] *La politique **ENVIRONNEMENTALE** de l'Union européenne repose sur la conviction que la croissance économique, le progrès social et la protection de l'environnement contribuent ensemble à l'amélioration de notre qualité de vie.* (Source : 1EUROPAENV)

[PT] *As empresas com performance **AMBIENTAL** são aquelas de maior inserção internacional, uma vez que neste ambiente a sensibilização dos problemas ambientais vem implicando uma maior pressão dos acionistas, consumidores e/ou órgãos de financiamento para uma nova postura empresarial.* (Source : SOCIEDADESUSTENTAVEL_1994)

iv) An indication of the reference to FrameNet with a hyperlink to FrameNet wherever relevant: the frame in focus has no reference to FrameNet; it was defined for the DiCoEnviro only.
• The list of participants (obligatory and optional ones): the participants listed are **Instrument**, **Cause** and **Means**, and they are all obligatory:
• The list of terms that evoke this frame in different languages: English (e.g. *clean*$_1$, *environmental*$_2$, *green*$_1$) French (e.g. *écologique*$_2$, *environnemental*$_2$, *proper*$_1$, *vert*$_1$) and Portuguese (e.g. *ambiental*$_2$, *ecológico*$_2$); the number on the right of each term indicates they are all entries in DiCoEnviro; hyperlinks to the DiCoEnviro are provided to visualize terminological entries and contextual annotations.

The last step, 'Definition of 'relations between frames', connects situations in different ways. For instance, the *Judgement_of_impact_on_the_environment* is linked via a See also relation with the *Recreation* frame (with terms such as en. *renewable*$_1$, fr. *renouvelable*$_1$, sp. *renovable*$_1$) and *Sustainability* frame (with terms such as en. *sustainability*$_1$; fr. *durable*$_1$; sp. *sostenibilidad*$_1$). Once linked, frames can lead to larger scenarios. For instance, *Sustainability* frame is linked via a property relation (is a property of) with Human_activity frame (with terms such as en. *activity*$_1$; fr. *activité*$_1$ and chinese 活动$_1$).

4. Specfic case analysis

By following the methodology we presented, the terminological analysis revealed how the linguistic behavior of terms may be unveiled and how this is effective for identifying the meaning of a term. Furthermore, this type of analysis supports meaning distinctions of the same lexical item.

In the analysis of the lexical item *ambiental*, some annotated contexts showed a different nature of semantic roles; this suggested we were probably dealing with two groups of terms and with two different meanings of a polysemous items, *ambiental*: 1. 'that concerns the environment' (as in environmental impact) and 2. 'that is designed to have minimum impact on the environment' (as in environ-mental policy). The following table shows how the meanings of the items are linked to different lexical units:

TERM	EXPLANATION	SHARED RELATIONS

[6] L'Homme (2020: 29-30) defined the explanation 'that is designed to have a minimum impact on the environment' for the adjectival terms that evoke this frame (e.g. en. *environmental*$_2$, fr. *environnemental*$_2$ fr. *écologique*$_2$, pt. *ambiental*$_2$, and others).

[7] L'Homme (2015: 38) presents an outline referring to each information given in the semantic frames.

ambiental$_1$	'that concerns the environment'	*ameaça*$_1$ ~, *crime* ~, *custo* ~, *dano* ~, *degradação*$_1$ ~, *desequilíbrio* ~, *destruição* ~, *ecológico*$_1$, *ambiental*$_2$, *meio ambiente*$_1$, en. *environmental*1, sp. *meioambiental*$_1$, fr. *environnemental*$_1$
ambiental$_2$	'that is designed to have minimum impact on the environment'	*atividade*$_1$ ~, *consciência* ~, *conservação*$_1$ ~, *educação* ~, *gestão* ~, *manejo*$_1$ ~, *performance* ~, *ecológico*$_2$, *ambiental*$_1$, *meio ambiente*$_1$, en. *environmental*$_2$, sp. *meioambiental*$_2$, fr. *environnemental*$_2$

Table 1: Relations shared by *ambiental* with other terms in the field of environment

Following we present the relations shared by *ambiental* in a graphical representation called *Neovisual*, a tool that provides access to the relations encoded in DiCoEnviro. The method used to develop this tool is described in L'Homme et al. (2018).

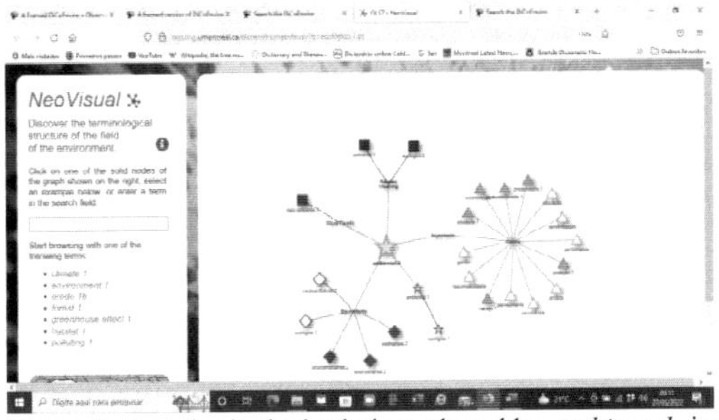

Figure 3. Terminological relations shared by *ambiental*$_2$ in Neovisual

The terminological relations we can extract from the graph are: i) the arguments of *ambiental*$_2$ (e.g. *atividade*$_1$ ~, *consciência* ~, *conservação*$_1$ ~, *educação* ~, *gestão* ~, *manejo*$_1$ ~, *performance* ~), ii) related meanings (e.g. *ecológico*$_2$, *ambiental*$_1$), iii) word family (e.g. *meio ambiente*$_1$), iv) equivalence (e.g. en. *environmental*$_2$, sp. *meioambiental*$_2$, fr. *environnemental*$_2$).

5. Conclusion

This article presented a terminological research carried out to account for terms of the environment in Brazilian Portuguese based on the lexico-semantic approach for Terminology (L'Homme, 2020). The descriptions are placed in two terminological resources, DiCoEnviro (2022) and Framed DiCoEnviro (2022). We showed that these resources are developed following a lexicon-driven approach that regards terms as lexical unit and intends to unveil the specialized knowledge in running texts. This perspective is innovative in terminological work developed in Brazilian Portuguese as existing resources on the environment usually present list of terms and multiword terms that shows no relations established among themselves. Based on two theoretical and methodological frameworks, ECL and Frame Semantics, the specialized meaning is captured based on the relations terms share with other terms. The analysis consists in delimiting the linguistic properties of terms, i.e. their predicative structure and lexical relations. This is also especially effective to support meaning distinctions as properties captured show different relations. The users of these resources are provided with entries that show a number of key information (e.g. argument structure, lexical relations, annotated contexts) and with semantic frames, evoked by specific terms, that characterize specialized knowledge on the environment. All this may be visualized both in textual format and in a graphical display (NeoVisual, 2022). The research reported here is ongoing. Portuguese has accounted for a total of 103 entries and 1.649 relations. Compared to other languages, especially French and English, we understand this work shall be expanded to unveil the specialized knowledge on the environment in Portuguese.

6. Acknowledgements

This work is supported by Fundação de Apoio à Pesquisa do Distrito Federal (FAP/DF), a research support institution of the Federal District in Brasília, Brazil. We would also like to thank the *Observatoire de Linguistique Sens-Texte* (OLST), at the University of Montreal, Canada, for providing the all the necessary means for the development of the terminological resources described here. We would also like to especially thank professor Marie-Claude L'Homme for providing useful feedback for this article.

7. Bibliographical References

Botta, M. G. (2013). Comportamento dos termos do meio ambiente em textos de vulgarização. *TradTerm*, 22(1):185-210.

Drouin, P. (2003). Term Extraction Using Non-Technical Corpora as a Point of Leverage. *Terminology*, 9(1): 99–117.

Fillmore, C. (1982). Frame Semantics. In Linguistics in the Morning Calm. The Linguistic Society of Korea. Seoul: Hanshin, pp.111-137.

Fillmore, C.J., and Baker, C. (2010). A Frames Approach to Semantic Analysis. In B. Heine and H. Narrog (Eds.), *The Oxford Handbook of Linguistic Analysis*. Oxford: Oxford University Press, pp. 313-339.

L'Homme, M.C. (2015). Découverte de cadres sémantiques dans le domaine de l'environnement: le cas de l'influence objective. *Terminàlia*, 12:29-40.

L'Homme, M. C. (2016). Terminologie de l'environnement et sémantique des cadres. SHS Web of Conferences, 5°. Congrès Mondial de Linguistique Française, France.

L'Homme, M. C.(2017). Maintaining the balance between knowledge and the lexicon in terminology: a methodology

based on Frame Semantics. *Lexicography, Journal of Asialex*, 4(1).
L'Homme, M. C., Robichaud, B. and Subirats, C. (2014). Discovering frames in specialized domains. In *Proceedings of the Ninth International Conference on Language Resources and Evaluation (LREC14)*. Reykjavik, Iceland.
L'Homme, M.C., Robichaud, B. and Prévil, N. (2018). Browsing the Terminological Structure of a Specialized Domain: A Method Based on Lexical Functions and their Classification. In *Language Resources and Evaluation, LREC 2018*. Myazaki, Japan.
L'Homme, M. C. (2020). *Lexical Semantics for Terminology: an introduction. Amsterdam/Philadelphia*. John Benjamins Publishing Company.
L'Homme, M. C., Robichaud, B., and Subirats, C. (2020). Building multilingual specialized resources based on FrameNet: Application to the field of the environment. *International FrameNet Workshop 2020. Towards a Global, Multilingual FrameNet*. Marseille, France.
Mel'čuk, I., Clas, A., and Polguère, A. (1995). *Introduction à la lexicologie explicative et combinatoire*. Duculot: Louvain-la-Neuve.
Pimentel, J. (2013). Methodological bases for assigning terminological equivalents. A Contribution. *Terminology*, 19(2): 237-257.
Polguère, A. (2016). *Lexicologie et sémantique lexicale* : notions fondamentales. Les Presses de l'Université de Montréal.
Ruppenhofer, J., Ellsworth, M., Petruck, M., Johnson, C., Baker, C. and Scheffczyk, S. (2016). FrameNet II: Extended Theory and Practice. (https://framenet.icsi.berkeley.edu/fndrupal/index.php?q =the_book).

8. Language Resource References

A Framed Version of DiCoEnviro (http://olst.ling.umontreal.ca/?page_id=2364) Accessed May 26, 2022.
Dicionário da copa de mundo (https://www.ufjf.br/framenetbr/dicionario/). Accessed May 26, 2022.
DiCoEnviro. Dictionnaire fondamental de l'environnement (http://olst.ling.umontreal.ca/cgi-bin/dicoenviro/search.cgi). Accessed May 26, 2022.
FrameNet (https://framenet.icsi.berkeley.edu/fndrupal/). Accessed May 26, 2022.
FrameNet Brasil. Juiz de Fora, MG: Universidade Federal de Juiz de Fora. (https://www.ufjf.br/framenetbr-eng/) Acessed May 26, 2022.
Glossário do Meio Ambiente (https://antigo.mma.gov.br/biodiversidade/biodiversidade-brasileira/gloss%C3%A1rio.html) Accessed May 20, 2022.
NeoVisual (http://olst.ling.umontreal.ca/dicoenviro/neovisual/) Accessed May 26, 2022.

Proceedings of the TERM21 Workshop , pages 8–12
Language Resources and Evaluation Conference (LREC 2022), Marseille, 20-25 June 2022

Knowledge Representation and Language Simplification of Human Rights

Sara Silecchia[1], Federica Vezzani[1], Giorgio Maria Di Nunzio[2]
[1] Department of Linguistic and Literary Studies, University of Padua, Italy
Via Elisabetta Vendramini, 13 - 35137 Padova - Italy
[2] Department of Information Engineering, University of Padua, Italy
Via Gradenigo, 6/a - 35131 Padova - Italy
sara.silecchia@studenti.unipd.it, [federica.vezzani, giorgiomaria.dinunzio]@unipd.it

Abstract: In this paper, we propose the description of a very recent interdisciplinary project aiming at analysing both the conceptual and linguistic dimensions of human rights terminology. This analysis will result in the form of a new knowledge-based multilingual terminological resource which is designed in order to meet the FAIR principles for Open Science and will serve, in the future, as a prototype for the development of a new software for the simplified rewriting of international legal texts relating to human rights, in order to facilitate their comprehension for non-expert people. Given the early stage of the project, we will focus on the description of its rationale, the planned workflow, and the theoretical approach which will be adopted to achieve the main goal of this ambitious research project.

Keywords: terminology, knowledge-based terminological resource, language simplification, Linked Open Data

1. Introduction

The current situation of worldwide conflicts has driven, once more, the attention to the problem of the interpretation of State responsibility for violations of Human Rights which has been debated for a long time in international law (Meron, T. 1989). This already thorny matter gets even more complicated given the ambivalent conception about the status of individuals in international law, since the traditional positivist doctrine considers States as the sole subjects of international law and individuals as the object (Salako, 2019). Nevertheless, this increasing involvement of individuals in international law is an interesting use case for the study of the language and terminology used to convey human rights granted under these circumstances. Given the specificity of its linguistic expression, we question whether the specialized language used to convey human rights is intelligible for legal laypeople.

In this context, legal specialized language has been extensively explored (see among others: Gémar, 1980; 1990; Dechamps, 2013; Biel, 2009; Cornu, 2005; Koelsch, 2016). In fact, difficulties for non-expert people in understanding legal language, often referred to as "legalese" (Melinkoff, 1963), have been widely debated and analyzed over the years (see among others: Charrow *et al.*, 1979; Tiersma, 1993; Masson *et al.*, 1994), to the extent that the calls for the simplification of legal writing led to the promotion of a "plain language". The most influential language-simplification efforts are attributed to the Plain English Movement in the US (Alterman, 1987; Benson, 1984; Benson *et al.*, 1987; Melinkoff, 1963; Wydick, 1978; 2005), which encouraged grammatical simplification of legal discourse due to the large number of impersonal utterances employed and the wide use of the passive voice (Richard, 2018), as well as its verbosity, complexities, and vagueness (Ződi, 2019), demanding its plain rewriting.

Nonetheless, others (Stark, 1994; Assy, 2011; Ződi, 2019) noted that the major simplicity and clarity of exposition claimed by the plain-legal-language movement fail to adequately represent the complexity of the law, as legal text comprehensibility seems not to be predominantly related to linguistic aspects. Ződi (2019) emphasized that sometimes, in legal drafting, clarity and accuracy can only be employed at "each other's expense", as legislative precision inevitably entails linguistic complexity.

Beyond any relevant theoretical position, this paper will focus on the description of a new research project aiming to provide a contribution in terms of clear representation and simplification of legal language, without any aim at demystifying law nor at diminishing the crucial role of lawyers as intermediaries between law and its subjects. The need to pursue such a study stem from laypeople's difficulties in understanding legal language and terminology and lies in the very nature of these rights: ensuring the enforcement of human and citizens' rights primarily requires their comprehension to be accessible for everyone through linguistic transparency.

The paper is organized as follows: in Section 2, we describe our research project specifically focusing on humanitarian rights terminology representation and simplification. We describe the main founding objectives as well as the planned workflow. In Section 3, we focus on the theoretical approach adopted in this research project for the conceptual and linguistic representation of human rights knowledge. Finally, Section 4 illustrates a first preliminary analysis conducted for the linguistic representation of the domain.

2. Research Project

The new interdisciplinary research project being discussed addresses the need to facilitate human rights comprehension for non-expert people, with the aim of proposing a methodology for the conceptual and multilingual linguistic representation of human rights and contributing to legal texts redrafting.

2.1 Objectives

The ultimate goal of this research project is the development of a new knowledge-based multilingual terminological resource, in which the data obtained will be structured based on the terminological record model provided in the FAIRterm Web application.[1] This tool is designed to offer the users the possibility to structure Findable, Accessible, Interoperable and Reusable terminological data and metadata, by following the latest ISO TC/37 SC 3 standards for terminology management (Vezzani, 2021).

This domain-specific terminological resource will serve as the basis for the development of a software prototype for redrafting legal texts. To this end, it is worth specifying that we intend to operate a "formal" simplification, as defined by Causa (2001), following which utterances are formally redrafted and no intervention is made at the content level.

2.2 Workflow

Our research approach will be structured as follows:

1) Specialized documents (namely international and national legal acts on human rights, including immigration rules) will be collected in three working languages: French, English, and Italian. Starting from this corpus, we will elaborate both a conceptual and a multilingual linguistic representation of human rights terminology, following Costa and Santos' mixed methodology for terminological knowledge representation (2015). The theoretical approach here adopted is hence based on the twofold nature of Terminology as consisting of a linguistic and a conceptual dimension. Subsequently, we will proceed with the identification of i) the concepts and their relationships; and then, for the three working languages, ii) the corresponding terms designating these concepts and their relationships, to assess whether a language-independent concept system can be overlapped with the multilingual lexical networks inferred from the purpose-built specialized corpus.
2) Once the double dimension of human rights terminology has been explored, from a multilingual perspective, the study will focus on the identification of terms, syntactic and grammatical structures related to specialized legal language and terminology that may hinder the comprehension of texts by legal laypeople's due to their linguistic opacity or their highly specialized status. This stage will be followed by the compilation of terminological records on the FAIRterm Web Application.
3) Based on the linguistic phenomena examined during the compilation of terminological records (synonymy, polysemy, hyponymy, and hypernymy), respective plain terms and syntactic or grammatical reformulations will be proposed as an alternative to non-transparent linguistic elements in the source texts.
4) Finally, we will perform an analysis and implementation on how to include the official identifiers and vocabularies (such as the European Legislation Identifier and European Case Law Identifier, and the European EuroVoc thesaurus[2]) in the TermBase eXchange (TBX) (ISO 30042:2019)[3] standard format of the terminological records.

2.3 A Linked Open Data "Open" Issue

An important aspect of this research proposal is the creation of a terminological resource which is reusable and interoperable. For these reasons, we will make use of both ISO standards of terminological databases (such TBX) as well as a Linked Open Data (LOD) paradigm, in more specifically the Linguistic Linked Open Data[4] paradigm, to publish data on the Web. In fact, LOD approaches give the researchers the possibility to design and implement open access tools to gather, study, and understand legal information. Despite having a wide variety of information publicly available online today, it is hard for a non-expert not only to understand the terminology and the language of laws (which is our primary focus) but also to cross-reference documents and the corresponding metadata. This problem can get even harder when legal documents from different jurisdictions are involved, such as legislative acts from the EU that influence national law, or in the case of cross-border cases. As discussed by Moodley et al. (2020), this gap between the legal and data proficiency that laypeople have can be the source for the development of software that is FAIR, publicly available, open-source, and easy to use by for anyone. In this sense, our research proposal for organizing and identifying legal terms according to the abovementioned ontologies, stems from the work of (Bacci et al. (2018), Linkoln; Filtz et al. (2021)) who propose an approach for the automatic extraction of legal references from legal texts and the enhancement of these data by means of legal knowledge graphs.

3. Theoretical Approach

In this section, we want to present the theoretical background of this work and the preliminary considerations about the linguistic representation of human rights.

3.1 Conceptual and Linguistic Dimension

The theoretical assumption underlying the proposed methodology lies in the dual nature of Terminology as composed of a conceptual and a linguistic dimension (Costa, 2013). Namely, Costa and Santos (2015) propose a methodology that combines both the onomasiological and the semasiological approach for terminological knowledge representation. This methodology is articulated in two stages: 1) the conceptual analysis of the Terminology of a domain, achieved without resorting to text analysis but by means of a domain concept map; 2) the linguistic analysis of the domain through the natural language processing tools, aiming at building a lexical network composed of terms and the relations to which they refer. In this context, the domain concept map would allow to eliminate ambiguity and adequately ensure coherence and consistency in domain representation for study purposes and validate the domain representation knowledge resulting from this structure.
Given the domain-independent nature of this dual approach, the expected objective is to apply this methodology of conceptual representation to the human rights domain.

[1] http://purl.org/fairterm
[2] https://eur-lex.europa.eu/browse/eurovoc.html
[3] https://www.iso.org/standard/62510.html
[4] https://linguistic-lod.org

3.2 Representation of Human Rights

As already mentioned, the knowledge representation of human rights does not serve solely for the purpose of terminological study, but the main objective being proposing a linguistic simplification of legal language, we believe that this type of approach would be the most appropriate to familiarise with the concepts concerned before carrying out any linguistic intervention for simplification purposes.

To perform Costa and Santos' analysis on the subject under study, and namely to identify the relevant concepts for study purposes, it is foreseen to consider mainly ontological relations as *part_of*, *connected_to*, *brings_about*, *occurs_in*, *carries_out*, *result_of*, *affects*, *process_of*, *uses*, or *exhibits*. The underlying objective is to make the relationships between legal concepts and their designations more explicit and to achieve greater clarity of exposition in legal texts primarily through conceptual clarity.

After the analysis of the concept system, a specialized corpus will be built by collecting specialized documents. The terminological extraction will then be carried out with the aim of retrieving the relevant terms based on their ``termhood'', that is the degree of detail to which a linguistic unit is related to specific concepts in a domain (Kageura and Umino, 1996). Subsequently, a map will be created by using the terms extracted from the corpus and directly related to the concepts in the map. At this stage, the analysis of the linguistic dimension is then performed through the identification markers, such as verbs, adverbs, or differentiation expressions, which introduce reformulations. As underlined by Costa *et al.* (2015), among others, lexical markers act as indicators of semantic relations (such as the cause/effect relation), and even punctuation is considered a linguistic marker. The assumption underlying this approach considers that for analysis purposes, not only terms are relevant but also other lexical units concur to build up the meaning of the discourse.

4. Preliminary analysis

In this section, we describe the initial analysis of the specialized language by performing the linguistic representation of the domain of human rights.

Being our final goal the creation of a multilingual resource, we decided to collect specialized documents in three working languages: English, French, and Italian. At this stage, we decided to have a parallel corpus consisting of all the international law treaties on human rights gathered from the official United Nations Human Rights Office of the Commissioner (UNHRC) archives[5], in addition to some of the international law instruments on human rights retrieved from the Council of Europe archive[6]. All these documents focus on international treaties on human rights, which embrace a broader spectrum of rights, such as civil, social, economic, and political rights, equally considered inherent to all human beings.

In order to collect and process these documents, we used Sketch Engine[7] (Kilgarriff et al., 2014). The current corpus is composed of 110 documents and 459,851 *tokens*. The keywords extraction function makes it possible to extract from the corpus the list of candidate terms of human rights domain, divided into single words, i.e. terms consisting of a single lexical unit, and multi-words, complex terms consisting of several units. The terminological extraction from the focus corpus is carried out through statistical calculations and analysis of the occurrences of candidate terms compared to the terminological data of a big pre-set reference corpus. Therefore, to make terminology extraction as selective and precise as possible, for each working language a specialized reference corpus has been selected. For the terminological extraction in Italian, the *EUR-Lex Italian 2/2016* reference corpus was chosen; in English two terminological extractions were made by combining the candidate terms extracted both from the *United Nations Parallel Corpus – English* and the *EUR-Lex English 2/2016*; whilst in French, the *United Nations Parallel Corpus – French* was selected, as the *EUR-Lex French 2/2016* was not available.

After this step, we performed a manual assessment of the extracted terms by means of the Concordance features in order to remove terms that are not relevant to the subject of study by looking at the context of occurrence and consequently to ascertain possible different connotations of terms within a particular context (for example, we removed multi-word terms like "concerning method of rehabilitation", "nouvelle convention portant revision" or "responsabilità delle persone").

A list of 790 terms for the three working languages are now under analysis for the subsequent description of the lexical networks of this domain.

One additional comment about this preliminary phase is the study of the polysemy and the different connotations of terms that have been observed during this preliminary analysis, Article 5 of the European Convention on Human Rights provides a clear example, in the authentic version in French and the respective Italian translation.

Article 5(c) in the French version[8] of the Convention mentions: "s'il a été arrêté et détenu en vue *d'être conduit* devant l'autorité judiciaire compétente [...]", which has been literally translated in the Italian text[9] of the Convention as "se è stato arrestato o detenuto *per essere tradotto* dinanzi all'autorità giudiziaria competente [...]". Whether the "expression *être conduit* devant l'autorité judiciaire" may be intuitive for French legal laypeople, the Italian translation "*essere tradotto* dinanzi all'autorità giudiziaria" is expected to appear harder. Indeed, in Italian, unlike the denotation of the term in standard language, indicating interlinguistic translation processes, in legal language the term "translation" means the transfer from one place to another of people under a regime of restriction of personal freedom. To adapt the linguistic expression of law to the needs of comprehension by a non-specialistic public, other alternative translations could be proposed, less opaque, but still consistent with the stylistic register of this domain, such as:

- "se è stato arrestato o detenuto per essere portato dinanzi all'autorità giudiziaria competente" ("if he has been arrested or detained to be brought before the competent judicial authority"); or

[5] https://www.ohchr.org/en/instruments-listings

[6] https://www.coe.int/en/web/conventions/full-list

[7] https://www.sketchengine.eu/

[8] https://www.echr.coe.int/documents/convention_fra.pdf

[9] https://www.echr.coe.int/documents/convention_ita.pdf

- “se è stato arrestato o detenuto affinché compaia dinanzi all'autorità giudiziaria competente” (“if he has been arrested or detained to appear before the competent judicial authority”).

Indeed, these alternative translations perfectly correspond to the English version of the mentioned article, the latter being: “the lawful arrest or detention of a person effected for the purpose of *bringing him* before the competent legal authority [...]”. Given the nature of the international convention and given that its effects concern also non-expert citizens, we believe that the proposed alternative translations meet the need for clarity of exposition and effective communication between international (and national) institutions and citizens, who, despite their lack of specific knowledge, are directly concerned by national and international standards.

5. Conclusions

Ensuring the enforcement of human and citizens' rights primarily requires their comprehension to be accessible for everyone through linguistic transparency. In order to achieve this objective, in this paper, we described the theoretical framework and the preliminary analysis of a research project that will 1) identify linguistic opacity related to legal specialized language that may hinder legal laypeople comprehension of international rules, 2) produce an open linguistic resource that follows the FAIR principles of open science. We believe that the proposed methodology and the design and implementation of the linguistic resource can effectively contribute to the improvement of human rights legislation understanding and drafting.

6. Acknowledgments

This work was partially supported by the ExaMode Project, as a part of the European Union Horizon 2020 Program under Grant 825292.

7. Bibliographical References

Alterman, I. (1987). Plain and Accurate Style in Court Papers. Philadelphia, PA: American Law Institute-American Bar Association Committee on Continuing Professional Education

Assy, R. (2011). Can the Law Speak Directly to Its Subjects? The Limitation of Plain Language. In *Journal of Law and Society*, Vol. 38, No. 3, pp. 376-404. URL: https://ssrn.com/abstract=1906372

Bacci, L., Agnoloni, T., Marchetti, C., Battistoni, R. (2018). Improving Public Access to Legislation through Legal Citations Detection: The Linkoln Project at the Italian Senate. *Law via the Internet.* 2018: 149-158. URL: https://ebooks.iospress.nl/publication/51783

Benson RW and Kessler JB. (1987). Legalese v. plain English: an empirical study of persuasion and credibility in appellate brief writing. In *Loyola of Los Angeles Law Review* 20, 301–321. URL: https://digitalcommons.lmu.edu/cgi/viewcontent.cgi?referer=&httpsredir=1&article=1493&context=llr

Benson, RW. (1984). The end of legalese: the game is over. New York University Review of Law and Social Change 13, 519–574. URL: https://socialchangenyu.com/wp-content/uploads/2019/09/ROBERT-W.-BENSON_RLSC_13.3.pdf

Biel, L. (2009). Corpus-Based Studies of Legal Language for Translation Purposes. In *Conference: Reconceptualizing LSP. Online proceedings of the XVII European LSP Symposium 2009*. Research Gate. URL: https://www.researchgate.net/publication/216576418_Corpus-Based_Studies_of_Legal_Language_for_Translation_Purposes

Causa, M. (2001). De la simplification en classe de français, langue professionnelle. In *Les Carnets du Cediscor*. URL : http://journals.openedition.org/cediscor/302 ; DOI : https://doi.org/10.4000/cediscor.302

Charrow, RP and Charrow, VR. (1979). Making Legal Language Understandable: A Psycholinguistic Study of Jury Instructions. In *Columbia Law Review*, 79(7), 1306–1374. https://doi.org/10.2307/1121842

Conceição, Manuel Célio. 2005. Concepts, termes et reformulations. Lyon: Presses Universitaires de Lyon

Cornu, G. (2005). Linguistique Juridique, Collection Domat / Droit privé, Montchrestien, 3eme édition

Costa, R., (2013), “Terminology and Specialised Lexicography: two complementary domains” in *Lexicographica* 29 (1), 29-42, 2013. 39, 2013.

Costa, R. and Santos, C. (2015). Domain specificity: semasiological and onomasiological knowledge representation. In Kockaert H. and Steurs F. (Eds.), *Handbook of Terminology (Vol. 1, pp. 153-179)*. John Benjamins Publishing Company, DOI: https://doi.org/10.075/hot.1.com1

Dechamps, C. (2013). L'enseignement du français juridique en centre de langues : quelques perspectives. In *Recherche et pratiques pédagogiques en langues de spécialité [Online], Vol. XXXIV N° 1* | 2015. URL: http://journals.openedition.org/apliut/5094; DOI: https://doi.org/10.4000/apliut.5094

Filtz, E., Kirrane, S., Polleres, A. (2021). The linked legal data landscape: linking legal data across different countries. In *Artif Intell Law* 29, 485–539 (2021). DOI: https://doi.org/10.1007/s10506-021-09282-8

Gémar, JC. (1980). La langue juridique, langue de spécialité au Québec: éléments de méthodologie. In *The French Review*, 53(6), 880–893. URL: http://www.jstor.org/stable/391928

Gémar, JC. (1990). Les fondements du langage du droit comme langue de spécialité. Du sens et de la forme du texte juridique. In *Revue générale de droit*, 21(4), 717–738. DOI : https://doi.org/10.7202/1058214ar

https://ebooks.iospress.nl/publication/51783

Gémar, JC. (2011). Aux sources de la “Jurilinguistique” : texte juridique, langues et cultures. In *Publications linguistiques* : Revue française de linguistique appliquée, 2011/1 Vol. XVI | pages 9 à 16, ISSN 1386-1204, URL : https://www.cairn.info/revue-francaise-de-linguistique-appliquee-2011-1-page-9.html

Lavault-Olléon, E., Grossmann, F. (2008). Langue du droit et harmonisation terminologique multilingue : l'exemple de LexALP. Lidil [En ligne], 38 URL : http://journals.openedition.org/lidil/2776 ; DOI : https://doi.org/10.4000/lidil.2776

Kageura, K., Umino, B. (1996) Methods of automatic term recognition: A review. In *Terminology. International Journal of Theoretical and Applied Issues* in Specialized Communication, Volume 3, Issue 2, Jan 1996, p. 259 – 289.

Kilgarriff, A., Baisa, V., Bušta, J. et al. (2014). The Sketch Engine: ten years on. Lexicography. In: *Asialex* 1, 7–36. DOI : https://doi.org/10.1007/s40607-014-0009-9

Koelsch, G. (2016). Specialized Language. In *Requirements Writing for System Engineering*. Apress, Berkeley, CA. DOI: https://doi.org/10.1007/978-1-4842-2099-3_3

Masson, M.E.J., Waldron, M.A. (1994). Comprehension of legal contracts by non-experts: Effectiveness of plain language redrafting. DOI: https://doi.org/10.1002/acp.2350080107

Melinkoff, D. (1963). The Language of the Law. In *Boston: Little Brown*.

Meron, T. "State Responsibility for Violations of Human Rights." *Proceedings of the Annual Meeting (American Society of International Law)* 83 (1989): 372–85. http://www.jstor.org/stable/25658498.

Moodley, K., Hernández Serrano, P., Zaveri, A., Schaper, M., Dumontier, M., Van Dijck, G. (2020). The Case for a Linked Data Research Engine for Legal Scholars. In *European Journal of Risk Regulation*, 11(1), 70-93. DOI: 10.1017/err.2019.51

Norme ISO 30042:2019. Gestion des ressources terminologiques – TermBase eXchange (TBX)., https://www.iso.org/fr/standard/62510.html

Richard, I. (2018). Is legal lexis a characteristic of legal language?". In *Lexis*. URL: http://journals.openedition.org/lexis/1173; DOI: https://doi.org/10.4000/lexis.1173

Salako, S. E. (2019). The Individual in International Law: 'Object' versus 'Subject'. In: International Law Research; Vol. 8, No. 1; 2019. ISSN 1927-5234 E-ISSN 1927-5242. Published by Canadian Center of Science and Education

Stark, J. (1994). Should the Main Goal of Statutory Drafting Be Accuracy or Clarity. In *Statute Law Review*, 15, 207-213. URL: https://doi.org/10.5539/ilr.v8n1p132

Tiersma, P. M. (1993). Reforming the Language of Jury Instructions. In *Hofstra Law Review: Vol. 22: Iss. 1*, Article 2. URL: http://scholarlycommons.law.hofstra.edu/hlr/vol22/iss1/2

Vezzani, F. (2021). La ressource FAIRterm : entre pratique pédagogique et professionnalisation en traduction spécialisée. In *Synergies Italie n° 17 – 2021*, p. 51-64, URL : https://gerflint.fr/Base/Italie17/vezzani.pdf

Wydick, R. C. (1978). Plain English for lawyers. In *California Law Review 66, 727–765*.

Wydick, R. C. (2005). Plain English for Lawyers, 5th edn. Durham, In *NC: Carolina Academic Press*.

Ződi, Z. (2019). The limits of plain legal language: understanding the comprehensible style in law. In *International Journal of Law in Context. 2019*. 246–262. 10.1017/S1744552319000260.

Proceedings of the TERM21 Workshop , pages 13–18
Language Resources and Evaluation Conference (LREC 2022), Marseille, 20-25 June 2022

Converting from the Nordic Terminological Record Format to the TBX Format

Maria Skeppstedt, Marie Mattson, Magnus Ahltorp, Rickard Domeij
Institute for Language and Folklore
Stockholm, Sweden
firstname.lastname@isof.se

Abstract

Rikstermbanken (Sweden's National Term Bank), which was launched in 2009, uses the Nordic Terminological Record Format (NTRF) for organising its terminological data. Since then, new terminology formats have been established as standards, e.g., the Termbase eXchange format (TBX). We here describe work carried out by the Institute for Language and Folklore within the Federated eTranslation TermBank Network Action. This network develops a technical infrastructure for facilitating sharing of terminology resources throughout Europe. To be able to share some of the term collections of Rikstermbanken within this network and export them to Eurotermbank, we have implemented a conversion from the Nordic Terminological Record Format, as used in Rikstermbanken, to the TBX format.

Keywords: Term banks, Nordic Terminological Record Format, TBX

1. Introduction

Rikstermbanken,[1] (Sweden's National Term Bank) was originally developed by "Terminologicentrum TNC" (The Swedish Centre for Terminology, TNC), which in 2006 was commissioned by the Swedish government to develop a national termbank (Nilsson, 2009; Bucher, 2009). The first technical implementation of Rikstermbanken was launched in 2009, and the product has since then been available through a search interface on a public website, which has been used by translators and terminologists at public agencies and other organisations in Sweden. The termbank hosts externally developed term collections, both from the public and private sector, as well as collections developed by TNC. Rikstermbanken contains both small and large term collections, with a total of 130,000 term entries, many of them multi-lingual.

When TNC closed down in the end of 2018, the responsibility of maintaining Rikstermbanken was handed over to ISOF (the Swedish Institute for Language and Folklore), i.e., the responsibility of maintaining the terminological content as well as the technical product. ISOF replaced the original Java and SQL-based implementation of Rikstermbanken in 2021 by a new technical implementation based on Python, Flask and the document database MongoDB.

According to the Language Act (Språklag (2009:600), 2009)[2] , the Swedish government agencies have the responsibility to ensure that terminology in their various areas of expertise is accessible, used and developed. ISOF provides the other agencies with support for implementing the Language Act, and Rikstermbanken forms one part of this work.

2. NTRF and TBX

The format chosen for storing the terminological data when developing the original version of Rikstermbanken was NTRF, the Nordic Terminological Record Format (Rådet for teknisk terminologi, 1999). This is a terminology format developed by central terminology institutions of Finland, Norway and Sweden. The standard NTRF version was adapted to requirements specific for the terminology data stored in Rikstermbanken to a local version of NTRF, which uses the fields shown in the first column of Table 2 for organising the data.

Since then, new terminology formats have been established as standards, e.g., the Termbase eXchange format (TBX) (Localization Industry Standards Association, 2008). TBX is an international standard for representation of structured terminological resources, and it defines an XML format for the exchange of terminology data. It is, for instance, used in terminology software and CAT tools (computer-assisted translation tools) to support the functionality of importing and exporting term lists.

There are also other possible formats, such as the SKOS format. However, as there are no hierarchical relations in the term collections in Rikstermbanken nor any linked data relations to entities outside of each term collection, we considered TBX to be the format most suitable to the data in Rikstermbanken.

Since Rikstermbanken was originally developed, it has also become more common that term collections are released as open data, and some of the term collections in Rikstermbanken are possible to release with an open license. These term collections are more useful to the third party user if they are made available in a standard

[1] `https://www.rikstermbanken.se`
[2] `https://www.riksdagen.se/sv/dokument-lagar/dokument/svensk-forfattningssamling/spraklag-2009600_sfs-2009-600`

format. They can then, for instance, easily be imported into a CAT tool or into other TBX-based termbanks. Therefore, to be able to share some of the data from Rikstermbanken in a standardised format, we have implemented a conversion from NTRF, as used in Rikstermbanken, to the TBX format.

2.1. An NTRF example

NTRF is a row-based format. Thereby, its structure is very different from the XML-based, hierarchical, TBX format. Table 1 shows the NTRF representation for the concept "biologisk mångfald" (biological diversity) from a collection of sustainability terms.[3]
The format also allows for expressing formatting of terms and texts, e.g., to express italics with HTML-like markup: {i}biologisk mångfald {/i}.

svTE biologisk mångfald
svSYTE biodiversitet
svUPTE artrikedom
enTE biological diversity
enSYTE biodiversity
svDF rikedom av arter, av genetisk variation inom arter samt av de ekosystem som arterna ingår i
svAN Begreppet biologisk mångfald betonar betydelsen av variationsrikedom bland alla levande organismer, exempelvis bakterier, växter, svampar och djur, samt de ekosystem och livsmiljöer de ingår i, allt från landskap med många olika naturtyper till städer med parker och grönområden.
I FN-fördraget "Konventionen om biologisk mångfald" definieras {i}biologisk mångfald {/i} som 'variationsrikedom bland levande organismer av alla ursprung, inklusive från bland annat landbaserade, marina och andra akvatiska ekosystem och de ekologiska komplex i vilka dessa organismer ingår; detta innefattar mångfald inom arter, mellan arter och av ekosystem'. Den definitionen används bland annat i juridiska sammanhang.
Benämningen {i}biologisk mångfald {/i} skiljer sig från det tidigare använda uttrycket {i}artrikedom{/i}, genom att det även avser den genetiska variationen inom en art
svEX Ett exempel på biologisk mångfald är när det finns olika arter av bin och humlor: jordhumlor, snäckmurarbin, tapetserarbin, honungsbin, fjällhumlor osv. De har olika kroppsform och längd på tunga, och olika preferenser när det gäller pollen och nektar, vilket innebär att de kan pollinera olika arter av växter.

Table 1: The NTRF representation for the concept "biologisk mångfald" (biological diversity) in Rikstermbanken.

Figure 1 shows how the term-post above is presented in the user interface of Rikstermbanken.

[3]The collection of sustainability terms, developed by the Institute for Language and Folklore, is licensed under a Creative Commons Attribution 4.0 International License, CC-BY 4.0 (http://creativecommons.org/licenses/by/4.0/)

3. The Federated eTranslation TermBank Network Action

The work of implementing a conversion from NTRF to TBX has been carried out within the Federated eTranslation TermBank Network Action, which is a network that develops a technical infrastructure for facilitating sharing of terminology resources throughout Europe. Among other initiatives, the network has implemented an API for pushing terminology resources in the TBX format from other termbanks into Eurotermbank. We will use this API and the TBX conversion described here for exporting some of Rikstermbanken's term collections to Eurotermbank[4].
In addition to the API for pushing terminology resources, the network has also implemented the Eurotermbank toolkit. This is a toolkit for managing terminology resources, i.e., for creating, editing, importing and exporting terminology in various formats. The toolkit is set up as a local web-based application, which functions as a local node that can export the terminology data to Eurotermbank. There are thus two main methods for exporting data into Eurotermbank, (i) either to use the API (i.e., the method ISOF uses), or (ii) to create or import terminology lists into a local node of the Eurotermbank toolkit.[5] The term lists exported to Eurotermbank are then exported further into the repository of the European Language Resource Coordination initiative, ELRC-SHARE[6]. This repository is used for training eTranslation[7], the machine translation system developed by the European Commission.
Figure 2 illustrates the conversion from NTRF to TBX and the export to Eurotermbank, and Figure 3 shows the term-post for "biologisk mångfald" (biological diversity) when it has been imported into Eurotermbank. Eurotermbank uses TBX 2.0, and this version was therefore chosen for the TBX export[8].

3.1. Term lists that are shared within the Federated eTranslation TermBank Network Action

The focus of the Federated eTranslation TermBank Network Action has been to construct and evaluate the technical infrastructure for sharing terminology resources, rather than to actually carry out the collection of resources to share. However, in order to practically evaluate the infrastructure, we have decided to start by exporting the following four resources from Rikstermbanken, with either a CC0 or a CC-BY license.

[4]https://www.eurotermbank.com
[5]Information on the network is available here: https://www.eurotermbank.com/participants-network
[6]https://elrc-share.eu
[7]https://ec.europa.eu/cefdigital/wiki/display/CEFDIGITAL/eTranslation
[8]With the following specification: https://eurotermbank.com/tbx-0.5.1.xcs

Termpost

SVENSKA TERMER:	**biologisk mångfald** biodiversitet
DEFINITION:	rikedom av arter, av genetisk variation inom arter samt av de ekosystem som arterna ingår i
ANMÄRKNING:	Begreppet biologisk mångfald betonar betydelsen av variationsrikedom bland alla levande organismer, exempelvis bakterier, växter, svampar och djur, samt de ekosystem och livsmiljöer de ingår i, allt från landskap med många olika naturtyper till städer med parker och grönområden. I FN-fördraget "Konventionen om biologisk mångfald" definieras *biologisk mångfald* som 'variationsrikedom bland levande organismer av alla ursprung, inklusive från bland annat landbaserade, marina och andra akvatiska ekosystem och de ekologiska komplex i vilka dessa organismer ingår; detta innefattar mångfald inom arter, mellan arter och av ekosystem'. Den definitionen används bland annat i juridiska sammanhang. Benämningen *biologisk mångfald* skiljer sig från det tidigare använda uttrycket *artrikedom*, genom att det även avser den genetiska variationen inom en art
EXEMPEL:	Ett exempel på biologisk mångfald är när det finns olika arter av bin och humlor: jordhumlor, snäckmurarbin, tapetserarbin, honungsbin, fjällhumlor osv. De har olika kroppsform och längd på tunga, och olika preferenser när det gäller pollen och nektar, vilket innebär att de kan pollinera olika arter av växter.
ENGELSKA TERMER:	biological diversity biodiversity
KÄLLA:	Hållbarhetstermgruppen: Termlista | 2021

Figure 1: The concept "biologisk mångfald" (biological diversity), as shown in Rikstermbanken (www.rikstermbanken.se).

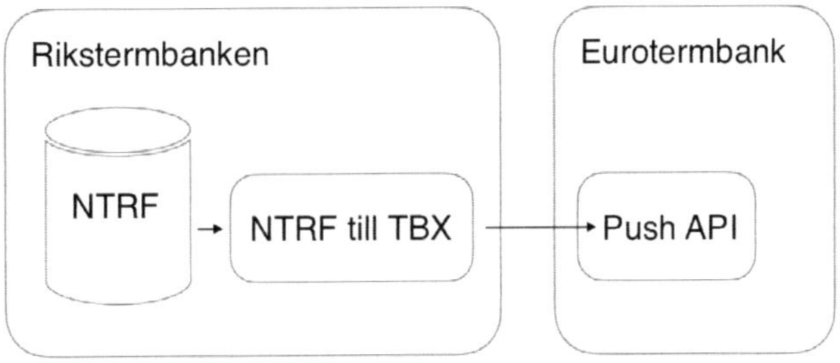

Figure 2: An illustration of the conversion from NTRF to TBX and the export to Eurotermbank

3.1.1. A collection of sustainability terms

ISOF organises the Sustainability Terminology Group, which aims to standardise and clarify Swedish terminology and concepts related to sustainable development. The group includes experts from a number of different knowledge areas, as well as actors who work to communicate such expert knowledge to a wider audience. The group members represent various scientific disciplines, government agencies, the media as well as NGOs. The linguistic expertise is provided by two terminologists and a discourse analyst, all from ISOF, as well as a translator from English to Swedish.

3.1.2. Terms from the Swedish authority terminology group

ISOF has also been organising a terminology group with the long-time goal of creating a more standardised terminology within the public sector. The terminology group included five different public agencies: the Swedish Tax Agency, the Swedish Public Employment Service, the Swedish Social Insurance Agency, the Swedish Police Authority and the National Board of Health and Welfare. The group members were terminologists, language experts, translators and business architects, and the group was led by a project manager, a project assistant and a terminologist from ISOF. The

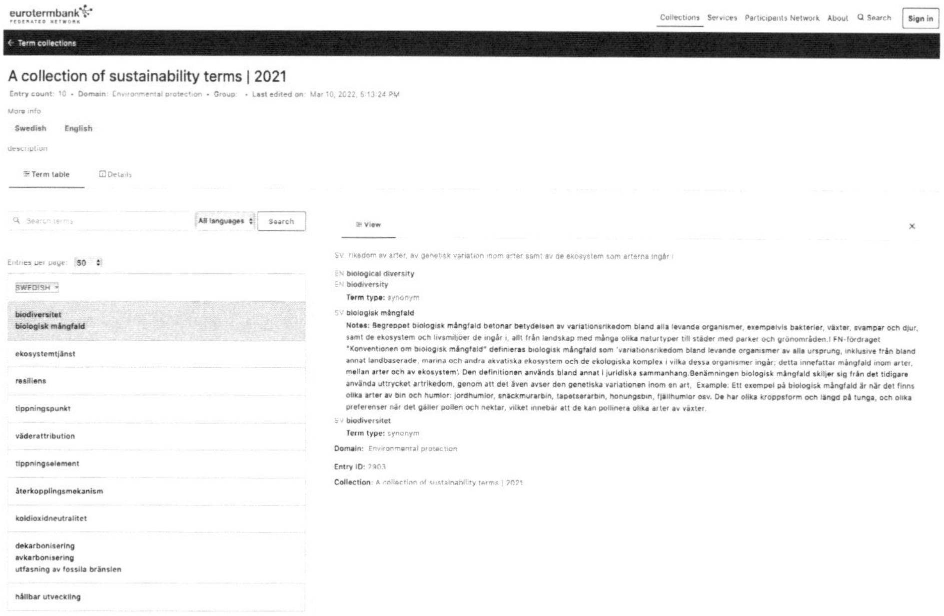

Figure 3: The concept "biological diversity" as shown when imported into Eurotermbank.

term list developed in the project consists of 27 term-posts, which are translated into five languages: English, Arabic, Finnish, Romani Arli and Romani Kelderash. The work began in August 2021 as a pilot project, but the group will hopefully continue to expand the terminology collection.

3.1.3. Statistics Sweden's term list

Statistics Sweden (SCB) is a public agency responsible for official statistics. Their term list, which contains terms in Swedish and English, consists of terms related to statistics, society, and other topics that can be useful when communicating statistics. The most recent update of the list was created by two statistics experts, two language experts and a terminologist consultant.

3.1.4. Swedish Council for Higher Education's term list

The Swedish Council for Higher Education (UHR) is responsible for supporting the higher education sector by providing admission services, IT systems, and the Swedish Scholastic Aptitude Test, among other things. Their term list consists of over 2,000 terms and synonyms related to higher education. The list is updated yearly with the help of institutions in the higher education sector.

4. The conversion

It could be concluded that the correspondence between NTRF and TBX in general was very good. There were only three pieces of information in NTRF that could not be directly expressed in TBX. These were (i) the Swedish common gender, (ii) domain on a language level, and (iii) translation equivalence comment on a language level. Table 2 shows a simplified mapping between the two formats, i.e., simplified in the way that the hierarchy of the TBX format has been left out. The pieces of information that can not be expressed in TBX are shown in boldface. The table is divided into the following five sections:

(2.1) TBX uses the hierarchical structure of XML to divide the term-post into language segments, whereas NTRF specifies the language for each term- and text row.

(2.2) NTRF allows the user to specify a number of different types of terms, e.g., standard term, synonym, deprecated term, whereas TBX uses the $<term>$ tag for all kinds of terms, and lets the user add additional tags to specify different kinds of term attributes, e.g., if it is a synonym or a deprecated term.

(2.3) For some features of the term, NTRF too uses attributes for specifying them, e.g., grammatical information, geographical usage, abbreviation/full form and homograph information. For all the attributes, there is a corresponding TBX tag. As stated above, we were, however, not able to find any standard in TBX for expressing that a noun has the common gender, which is one of the gender categories of Swedish. Terms having another gender category than "feminine", "masculine" and "neuter" were therefore given the gender category "othergender".

(2.4) There is also information on a language level, both for NTRF and TBX, e.g., a definition or explanation of the concept, or a note. These pieces of information can optionally have a reference. On the lan-

NTRF	TBX
1. The language:	
la	<langSet xml:lang=*la*> … (where *la* is a variable containing the language)
2. The term:	
*la*TE *word*	<term>*word*</term> …
*la*AVTE *word*	<term>*word*</term> … <termNote type="normativeAuthorization">deprecatedTerm</termNote> <termNote type="administrativeStatus">deprecatedTerm-admn-sts</termNote>
*la*BT *word*	<term>*word*</term> … <termNote type="termType">formula</termNote>
*la*PH *word*	<term>*word*</term> … <termNote type="termType">phraseologicalUnit</termNote>
*la*SYPH *word*	<term>*word*</term> … <termNote type="termType">synonym</termNote> <termNote type="termType">synonymousPhrase</termNote> <termNote type="termType">phraseologicalUnit</termNote>
*la*SYTE *word*	<term>*word*</term> … <termNote type="termType">synonym</termNote>
*la*INTE *word*	<term>*word*</term> … <termNote type="termType">fullForm</termNote>
Also for: *la*TE and *la*PH	(If the setting 'troligenUppdelat' ('probably split') is true for the language:) <termNote type="normativeAuthorization">preferredTerm</termNote> <termNote type="administrativeStatus">preferredTerm-admn-sts</termNote>
Also for: *la*SYPH and *la*SYTE	(If the setting 'troligenUppdelat' ('probably split') is true for the language:) <termNote type="normativeAuthorization">admittedTerm</termNote> <termNote type="administrativeStatus">admittedTerm-admn-sts</termNote>
3. Information associated with the term:	
GNGR f	<termNote type="grammaticalGender">feminine</termNote>
GNGR m	<termNote type="grammaticalGender">masculine</termNote>
GNGR t	<termNote type="grammaticalGender">neuter</termNote>
GNGR **other**	<termNote type="grammaticalGender">**otherGender**</termNote> (Can, e.g., be used for Swedish common gender, which is not expressed in TBX.)
GR pl	<termNote type="grammaticalNumber">plural</termNote>
GR sing	<termNote type="grammaticalNumber">singular</termNote>
GR koll	<termNote type="grammaticalNumber">mass</termNote>
another GR	<termNote type="grammaticalNumber">otherNumber</termNote>
OKGR subst	<termNote type="partOfSpeech">noun</termNote>
OKGR adj	<termNote type="partOfSpeech">adjective</termNote>
OKGR verb	<termNote type="partOfSpeech">verb</termNote>
OKGR adv	<termNote type="partOfSpeech">adverb</termNote>
OKGR itr	<termNote type="partOfSpeech">verb</termNote> <termNote type="grammaticalValency">monovalent</termNote>
OKGR tr	<termNote type="partOfSpeech">verb</termNote> <termNote type="grammaticalValency">divalent or more</termNote>
another OKGR	<termNote type="partOfSpeech">other</termNote>
FRKT F	<termNote type="termType">abbreviation</termNote>
FRKT OF	<termNote type="termType">fullForm</termNote>
HONR *nr*	<termNote type="homograph">*nr*</termNote>
UT *text*	<termNote type="pronunciation">*text*</termNote>
RF *text*	<xref type="xSource" target=" *text* " />
SA *text*	<termNote type="usageNote">*text*</termNote>
GE *text*	<termNote type="geographicalUsage">*text*</termNote>
EKVI *text*	<termNote type="transferComment">*text*</termNote> (EKVI is currently not used in Rikstermbanken on a term level.)
4. Information associated with the language:	
*la*DF *text*	<descrip type="definition">*text*</descrip>
*la*EX *text*	<descrip type="example">*text*</descrip>
*la*FK *text*	<descrip type="explanation">*text*</descrip>
*la*KT *text*	<descrip type="context">*text*</descrip>
la{DF/EX/FK/KT} *text* RF *text*	(The four preceding text attributes can also be given an optional reference) <descrip type="{definition/example/explanation/context}">*text*</descrip> <admin type="sourceIdentifier">*text*</admin>
*la*AN *text*	<note>*text*</note>
*la*AN *text.1* RF *text.2*	(In addition, if there is a reference associated with the note) <admin type="annotatedNote">*text.1*</admin> <adminNote type="noteSource">*text.2*</adminNote>
***la*SA** *text*	<note>**Domain:** *text*</note>
***la*EKVI** *text*	<note>**Equivalence:** *text*</note>
*la*UPTE *w.1, w.2*	<admin type="searchTerm">*w.1*</admin> <admin type="searchTerm">*w.2*</admin>
5. References to other terms, which are associated with the language in NTRF and with the term-post in TBX:	
*la*RETE *word* (<HONR *nr*>)	<ref type="crossReference" target="*word(-nr)*">*word*</ref> (A homograph number is needed when referencing to homographs)
*la*SU *word* (<HONR *nr*>)	<ref type="see" target="*word(-nr)*">*word*</ref> (A homograph number is be needed when referencing to homographs)

Table 2: A simplified mapping table between Rikstermbanken NTRF and TBX, not showing the hierarchical structure of the TBX. *la* is variable containing the language, *word* (and *w.1/w.2*) contains a word, *text* contains a text, and *nr* contains a number. The three pieces of information in NTRF that could not be expressed in TBX is shown in boldface.

guage level, both NTRF and TBX also lets the user specify search words, i.e., words that should lead to this term-post being retrieved when used in a search query. NTRF also allows the user to specify a "translation equivalence comment" as well as a "domain" on the language level. We have not been able to find support for adding this information on the language level in TBX, and have therefore instead added a standard TBX note that starts with the text "Domain:" and "Equivalence:", respectively. This is shown in boldface in the table.
(2.5) Finally, related terms and see-under terms are expressed on a language level in NTRF, whereas they are expressed with XML tags on a term-post level in TBX. We moved the information to the term-post level when carrying out the conversion.
The typographic formatting of the text and terms, i.e., the HTML-like markup, is not exported in the current implementation of the conversion.
The conversion is implemented in Python. The conversion procedure consists of first retrieving the NTRF formatted files from their representation in the document database, and thereafter converting them into TBX.

5. Future work

In the future, we will continue to select term lists from Rikstermbanken to export to Eurotermbank, as well as to develop and collect new term lists to include in Rikstermbanken.
We plan to continue to support NTRF for Rikstermbanken, as there is knowledge within ISOF on how to use this format. We have, however, also implemented the first stage of a conversion in the other direction, i.e., a conversion *from* TBX. Such a conversion would make it possible to import data available in a TBX format into the MongoDB database of Rikstermbanken, i.e., making the TBX format one of the formats supported for importing data into Rikstermbanken.

6. Acknowledgements

The Federated eTranslation TermBank Network Action is co-financed by the Connecting Europe Facility of the European Union.
The contents of this paper are the sole responsibility of the authors and do not necessarily reflect the opinion of the European Union.

7. Bibliographical References

Bucher, A.-L. (2009). Terminologisamordning inom svenska myndigheter ny språklag på väg. In *NORDTERM16: Ontologier og taksonomier.*

Localization Industry Standards Association. (2008). Systems to manage terminology, knowledge, and content - termbase exchange (TBX). https://www.gala-global.org/sites/default/files/migrated-pages/docs/tbx_oscar_0.pdf.

Nilsson, H. (2009). The realisation of a national term bank – how and why? In *ELETO – 7th Conference Hellenic Language and Terminology.*

Rådet for teknisk terminologi. (1999). Nordic terminological record format (NTRF).

Språklag (2009:600). (2009). Kulturdepartementet.

Proceedings of the TERM21 Workshop , pages 19–25
Language Resources and Evaluation Conference (LREC 2022), Marseille, 20-25 June 2022

A Dataset for Term Extraction in Hindi

Shubhanker Banerjee, Bharathi Raja Chakravarthi, John Philip McCrae
ADAPT Centre
National University Of Ireland Galway
shubhanker.banerjee@adaptcentre.ie

Abstract

Automatic Term Extraction (ATE) is one of the core problems in natural language processing and forms a key component of text mining pipelines of domain specific corpora. Complex low-level tasks such as machine translation and summarization for domain specific texts necessitate the use of term extraction systems. However, the development of these systems requires the use of large annotated datasets and thus there has been little progress made on this front for under-resourced languages. As a part of ongoing research, we present a dataset for term extraction from Hindi texts in this paper. To the best of our knowledge, this is the first dataset that provides term annotated documents for Hindi. Furthermore, we have evaluated this dataset on statistical term extraction methods and the results obtained indicate the problems associated with development of term extractors for under-resourced languages.

Keywords: automatic term extraction, under-resourced, Hindi

1. Introduction

Automatic Term Extraction (ATE) is the task of extracting relevant terms from domain specific corpora. Terms can be defined as linguistic units that refer to domain specific concepts in a world model (Cabré, 1999; Cram and Daille, 2016; Peñas et al., 2001b). To illustrate, in the domain of education an institution that imparts education to children is a concept and we refer to this concept by the word *school* in English. Thus, identification of a word or a multiword expression as a term is highly dependent on the individual's subjective notion of the concept (Peñas et al., 2001b), for example how does the individual define education and whether institution is an important concept in this domain as per the subjective opinion of the person. This in turn makes ATE a more challenging problem to tackle.

Term extractors also play a critical role in ontology engineering as identification of terms and relationships amongst them can be used to identify important concepts and conceptual relations which in turn serve as building blocks for ontologies (Pazienza et al., 2005). They are also used in the development of language technology such as machine translation (Oliver, 2017) and summarization systems (Jacquemin and Bourigault, 2005). Furthermore, they serve as the key building blocks of information retrieval systems as they allow efficient indexing of relevant documents (Jacquemin and Bourigault, 2005) together on the basis of terms thus playing a critical role in reducing the overall search time and improving the scalability of these systems.

Although term extraction has been an active area of research in the past few decades, most of the research in this domain has primarily been focused on English (Pazienza et al., 2005; Šajatović et al., 2019; Astrakhantsev, 2018; Zhang et al., 2018). Out of the 7,100+ languages[1] being used around the world most are under-resourced with limited access to language technology tools. In this paper, we present a novel dataset for term extraction in the education domain for the Hindi language. Furthermore, we have carried out experiments with statistical term extraction systems on this dataset to demonstrate the challenges in building term extractors. We hope that by releasing this dataset we can contribute towards the research in resource creation as well as development of better algorithms for term extraction for under-resourced languages.

The related works have been discussed in Section 2, Section 3 details the dataset collection techniques as well as processing carried before conducting the experiments. Furthermore, we go onto list the data statistics in terms of the total number of annotated documents and the methodology followed while annotating the documents. The algorithms used to carry out the experiments are discussed in Section 4 followed by a discussion on the evaluation metric and the experiments in Section 5 and Section 6 which reviews the results obtained. Lastly, future directions of research and open problems are described in Section 7.

2. Related Works

ATE has been an active area of research since the last decade of the previous millennium (Daille, 1994; Evans and Lefferts, 1995; Pazienza, 1998) with almost all of the research in this domain being focused on statistical techniques; both supervised and unsupervised.

[1] `https://www.ethnologue.com/`

Earlier research in this domain was focused around frequency based measures such as Term Frequency - Inverse Document Frequency (TF-IDF) (Evans and Lefferts, 1995) and linguistic filter based methods (Daille, 1994). The key idea behind the TF-IDF based methods is that terms representative of important concepts have high document term frequency in a few documents. The methods based on linguistic filtering exploit general syntactic patterns observed in terms across domains for example associating noun phrases with terms. Bordea et al. (2013) propose a term recognition algorithm based on the the identification of termhood of the term constituents. In recent years, this ongoing research has culminated in the form of various term extraction toolkits, namely: TermSuite (Cram and Daille, 2016), Simple Extractor[2], SDL MultiTerm Extract[3], Terminus[4], JATE (Zhang et al., 2016), Rainbow [5] and ATR4S (Astrakhantsev, 2018) which have advanced the state-of-the-art in term extraction tasks.

The experiments carried out in this paper are based on the frequency based algorithms demonstrated by Astrakhantsev (2018). They carry out experiments with various methods such as methods based on occurrence frequency, methods based on topic modelling and context modelling based methods.

Term annotated datasets are available for popular highly resourced languages such as English, however not a lot of progress has been made with regards to curation of term annotated datasets for under-resourced languages. GENIA (Kim et al., 2003) is term annotated dataset for the domain of biomedicine in English. It contains 2000 abstracts taken from the MEDLINE database comprising of over 400,000 tokens and annotated with 93,293 terms. The CRAFT corpus (Bada et al., 2012), belonging to the biomedical domain is another popular term annotated dataset for domain specific terminology in English. Similary, there are other datasets available for English such as ACL RD-TEC (?) and ACTER [6]. This research is closely related to the work done by McCrae and Doyle (2019) who introduce a term annotated dataset for Irish (ISO 639-3 language code for Irish is gle), an under-resourced language of the Goidelic family of languages. The Goidelic languages are a part of the larger Celtic family of languages used primarily in the British Isles. Irish, Scottish Gaelic and Manx are the 3 languages which constitute the Goidelic family. They demonstrate term extraction on this dataset using various methods such as frequency based measures and topic modelling based approaches. Also, they propose the inclusion of morphological features in the term recognition pipeline in order to improve the performance of the statistical term recognition system. In this paper, we have used frequency and background corpus based measures for term extraction.

2.1. Hindi

Hindi is an under-resourced language from the Indo-European family of languages primarily used in the northern and north-western parts of the Indian subcontinent (Kachru, 2006). There are 528 million native speakers of the language in the Indian subcontinent as per the census of 2011 conducted by the Government of India[7]. Hindi is written in the Devanagari script which is a phonetic script; the writing system reflects the pronunciations (Bright, 1996). For example, dog is written as श्वान in Hindi and prounounced as *shvaan*.

3. Dataset

The dataset introduced in this paper is a collection of documents from the domain of education. The choice of this particular domain is not due to a specific scientific reason but influenced by the authors' expertise in this domain by virtue of previous and current academic affiliations. Data required for annotation has been collected from Wikipedia using its standard api [8]. A total of 71 Wikipedia documents comprising of 11,960 words were collected and manually annotated. Wikipedia pages are classified into categories to group pages from the same domain together. In Hindi Wikipedia, category is known as श्रेणी (transliteration - shreni, translation - category) and setting this parameter to शिक्षा (transliteration - shiksha, translation - education) in the API GET request enables us to download the documents belonging to this domain. During annotation we referred to the fundamental definition of a term: *term is a surface representation of a concept* (Pazienza, 1998). Of course, the definition of concepts is subjective and reflects the annotators' notion of termhood in the given domain. It is also important note that we haven't posed any syntactic structure on term selection. This has been done to increase the coverage and allow the terms representative of a variety of different concepts to be annotated. However, during

[2]`https://www.dail.es/en/artificial-intelligence/`

[3]`https://docs.rws.com/binary/796827/807059/sdl-multiterm-2021-sr1/sdl-multiterm-extract-tools-user-guide`

[4]`http://terminus.iula.upf.edu/cgi-bin/terminus2.0/terminus.pl?lInt=En`

[5]`https://okapiframework.org/wiki/index.php/Rainbow`

[6]`https://clarin.eurac.edu/repository/xmlui/handle/20.500.12124/24`

[7]`https://censusindia.gov.in/2011Census/Language_MTs.html`

[8]`https://hi.wikipedia.org/w/api.php`

annotation we observed that almost all the annotated terms are noun phrases. In fact, a total of 926 annotated terms were noun phrases, 25 verb phrases were annotated as terms and 2 adjectives were also annotated as terms. As a part of the data cleaning, the English words in the downloaded data have been filtered out using a unicode based character filtration.

A total of 71 documents were annotated with 953 terms. Also, it is also important to note that the annotation was performed by a single annotator. For under-resourced languages like Hindi, it is difficult to onboard trained expert annotators due to the scarcity of domain experts and high expenses associated with their recruitment. In this case these challenges have limited the size of the dataset and since the dataset has been manually annotated by one annotator therefore it is difficult to ascertain the quality of annotations and the possibility of noisy annotation cannot be ruled out.

The aforementioned problems with manual annotation can hinder the learning of any meaningful representations and lead to degraded performance in the supervised learning domain. However, self-supervised learning algorithms which are robust to noisy annotation and can learn meaningful representations by seeding on the initial annotated dataset (Tan et al., 2021) can be used to train machine learning models for the task at hand.

Lastly, although the size of the dataset is relatively small, we hope that it can propel research interest in this domain for the Hindi language. The dataset and necessary code developed during its curation are available publicly [9].

4. Methodology

We evaluated the performance of frequency and reference corpora based term extraction approaches discussed by Astrakhantsev (2018) using the dataset introduced in Section 3 as the gold standard. The following are the steps involved in the term extraction pipeline:

- Pre-processing
- Term candidate selection
- Term candidate scoring and ranking[10]

The methods detailed in sections 4.2.3, 4.2.4 and 4.2.5 are based on a general domain background corpus. We used 2,411 Wikipedia articles comprising of 7,28,055 words spread across multiple domains as our background corpus [11].

[9] `https://github.com/zigzagthad/Hindi_Term-Extract`

[10] In this paper, we have used one method for term scoring therefore ranking is trivial. However, in methods where multiple term scoring methodologies are involved, term ranking becomes complicated.

[11] `https://rb.gy/d5o4yi`

4.1. Term Candidate Selection

We used part-of-speech chunking for filtering the term candidates. Firstly, we annotated the documents with the TnT tagger (Brants, 2000) which is available as a part of the NLTK package. Next, we used the RegexpParser also available as a part of the NLTK package to perform chunking on the annotated documents. Precisely, all noun phrases were considered as term candidates to be scored using the methods discussed in the subsequent sections. Here it is important to note that the tnt tagger for the Hindi language is trained on 540 annotated sequences. This impedes the performance of the part-of-speech tagging step and reflects resource constraints in under-resourced scenarios.

Also, it was ensured that the selected term candidates have a length of at least 3 and in case of multi-word expressions it was ensured that all individual words constituting the expression have a length of 3 at least.

4.2. Term Scoring and Ranking

The term candidates selected in the previous step were scored with the following 5 different methods as proposed by (Astrakhantsev, 2018):

- Term Frequency - Inverse Document Frequency (TF-IDF)
- Residual Inverse Document Frequency (RIDF)
- Domain Pertinence
- Weirdness
- Relevance

For a particular scoring algorithm the term candidates were ranked in decreasing order of the scores achieved by them.

4.2.1. TF-IDF

As a part of the experiments, we carried out term scoring using the term frequency-inverse document frequency algorithm (Evans and Lefferts, 1995). It's an information retrieval algorithm that assigns higher values to terms that have high occurrence frequency in a few documents according to Equation 1. The intuition behind using this algorithm for term extraction is that terms that represent concepts in a specific domain have a high occurrence frequency in the domain-specific documents.

$$TF \cdot IDF(t) = TF(t) \cdot \log_2 \frac{D}{DTF(t)} \quad (1)$$

where TF(t) is the term frequency, D is the total number of document in the collection, DTF(t) is a number of documents in which the term occurs.

4.2.2. RIDF

The RIDF algorithm first proposed by (Church and Gale, 1999) was used by (Zhang et al., 2016) for term extraction. The key idea behind using this approach for term extraction is that the IDF that is observed for terms has a greater deviation from a standard Poisson deviation as compared to the deviation observed for non-terms as shown in Equation 2.

$$RIDF(t) = TF(t) \cdot \log_2 \frac{D}{DTF(t)} + \log_2(1 - e^{-ATF(t)}) \quad (2)$$

where ATF is the normalized term frequency, normalized the number of documents in which a term occurs.

4.2.3. Domain Pertinence

Domain pertinence (Meijer et al., 2014) is a background corpus based term extraction method. The key idea behind background corpus based methods is that terms in a domain specific collection are different from non-terms with regards to their occurrence statistics in a background collection. Equation 3 shows the calculation of Domain pertinence for linguistic units in a domain specific corpus. For a specific term candidate, domain pertinence is calculated as a ratio of term frequency in the given corpus and the term frequency in the background corpus.

$$DomainPertinence(t) = \frac{TF_{target}(t)}{TF_{reference}(t)} \quad (3)$$

where TF_{target} is the term frequency in the domain specific corpus and $TF_{reference}$ is the term frequency in the general background corpus.

4.2.4. Weirdness

Khurshid et al. (2000) normalizes the term frequencies by the total number of the words in the respective collection.

$$Weirdness(t) = \frac{NTF_{target}(t)}{NTF_{reference}(t)} \quad (4)$$

where NTF_{target} is the term frequency in the domain specific corpus normalized by the total number of words in the domain specific corpus and $NTF_{reference}$ is the term frequency in the general background corpus normalized by the total number of words in the background corpus.

4.2.5. Relevance

(Peñas et al., 2001a) is a modification to domain pertinence and the weirdness algorithm as it takes into account document frequency in the calculation, that is the number of documents in which a term occurs.

$$Relevance(t) = 1 - (\log_2(2 + \frac{NTF_{target}(t) \cdot DF_{target}(t)}{NTF_{reference}(t)}))^{-1} \quad (5)$$

where NTF_{target} is the term frequency in the domain specific corpus normalized by the total number of words in the domain specific corpus and $NTF_{reference}$ is the term frequency in the general background corpus normalized by the total number of words in the background corpus and DF_{target} is the number of documents in the domain corpus in which a term occurs.

5. Experiments

Term extraction can be viewed as a retrieval of terms from text documents. There are primarily two kinds of retrieval evaluation algorithms, namely ranked and unranked (Manning et al., 2010) evaluation metrics. Unranked evaluation metrics don't take into account the relative ranks of the term candidates, that is the score attained by the term candidates as per scoring algorithms does not contribute to the evaluation. On the contrary, these metrics are evaluated on the basis of term candidate lists returned by the retrieval algorithm (in this case the chunker). In this paper, we have used 3 unranked evaluation algorithms namely Precision, Recall and F1 score. Precision essentially calculates the proportion of relevant terms out of the total number of retrieved terms (Manning et al., 2010) as given in Equation 6

$$Precision = \frac{Number\ of\ relevant\ items\ retrieved}{Total\ number\ of\ retrieved\ items} \quad (6)$$

Recall calculates the proportion of relevant terms out of the total number of relevant terms (Manning et al., 2010) as given in Equation 7

$$Recall = \frac{Number\ of\ relevant\ items\ retrieved}{Total\ number\ of\ relevant\ items} \quad (7)$$

F1-score is an unranked evaluation score that is calculated as the harmonic mean of Precision and Recall (Manning et al., 2010). Relative ranks of the term candidates don't contribute towards the calculation of these scores and therefore their values are same across different scoring algorithms and are illustrated in Table 1.

Ranked evaluation algorithms on the other hand take into account the score generated by the scoring algorithm and calculate the metric for the most relevant terms(ones with the highest score). The key idea behind these metrics is that the user is interested in the top k terms out of the complete term list returned by the filter (chunker in this case).

Table 1: Unranked Evaluation Results

Precision	Recall	F1
0.106	0.023	0.037

Table 2: Ranked Evaluation Results

Algorithm	MAP	MAR	MAF1
TF-IDF	0.079	0.016	0.031
RIDF	0.079	0.016	0.031
Domain Pertinence	0.091	0.018	0.037
Weirdness	0.091	0.018	0.037
Relevance	0.089	0.018	0.036

In this paper we have used k = 5 for evaluation of the metrics. This means that the metrics are evaluated for each of the top-5 terms in the list of retrieved term candidadates sorted in decreasing order of their scores. In cases where the total size of the term list returned by the filter is less than 5 then we have set k = length of the filtered term candidate list.

As a part of the experiments we have used 3 different ranked evaluation metrics namely Mean Average Precision (MAP), Mean Average Recall (MAR) and Mean Average F1-score (MAF1). MAP is the mean of Average Precision@k (AP@k given by Equation 8) over all the documents of the collection. Similarly, MAR is the mean of Average Recall@k (AR@k given by Equation 9) over all the documents of the corpus. MAF1 is the harmonic mean of AP@k and AR@k over all the documents in the collection.

$$Average\ Precision(k) = \sum_{i=1}^{k} \frac{\frac{TP@i}{TP@i+FP@i}}{k} \quad (8)$$

$$Average\ Recall(k) = \sum_{i=1}^{k} \frac{\frac{TP@i}{TP@i+FN@i}}{k} \quad (9)$$

where TP is the number of true positives, FP is the number of false positives and FN is the number of false negatives.

6. Results and Discussion

The results obtained are illustrated in Table 1 and Table 2. As can be seen the scores for all the algorithms are not very high. Furthermore, it can be observed that the values for precision are higher than the recall values for both ranked and unranked evaluation metrics. This is primarily due to the sub-optimal selection of term candidates for each document. As discussed previously the term candidates were filtered by first annotating the documents with the tnt tagger, followed by chunking performed using the RegexpParser (both tnt tagger and RegexpParser are available as a part of the NLTK package) to select the noun phrases as term candidates. However it was observed that tagger had limited capacity and a large number of chunks were annotated with *<UNK>* tokens (unknown tokens). As a result a very low number of term candidates (noun phrases) were filtered for each document which in turn brought down the recall scores leading to very high false negatives.

It is also interesting to note that the values for the ranked metrics is lower is than the values for the unranked metrics which indicates that scoring algorithms don't reflect the gold standard lists; they assign higher ranks to non-term entities. There are two possible reasons for this; firstly, the list of filtered term candidates is not representative of the gold standard and as result the performance is low irrespective of the rank assigned by the scoring algorithm; and secondly another reason could be that termhood in this domain is not reflected by frequency of occurrence. However, on closer inspection of the results we found that where an appropriate list of term candidates had been filtered out, the term scores were high and which in turn indicated that term candidates have high occurrence frequency in both the target as well as the background corpus thus ruling out the possibility of the second reason mentioned previously.

Furthermore, as illustrated in Table 2 algorithms belonging to the same class; frequency based approaches namely TF-IDF and RIDF exhibit similar performance and similarly background corpus based approaches namely Domain Pertinence, Weirdness and Relevance have similar performance. This is because of similar ranking patterns across a specific class of algorithms.

Also, it is interesting to note that background corpus based methods have a slightly better performance than the frequency based approaches, this is indicative of the positive influence of the background corpus on the task at hand.

7. Conclusion and Future Work

To conclude the dataset described here is the first term annotated dataset for Hindi. During evaluation of this dataset with unsupervised algorithms we observed that the score of frequency and background corpus based methods is not high. As discussed previously, this is primarily due to the suboptimal performance of tagger leading to inefficient selection of term candidates. Another important aspect is the search criteria for chunking, introduction of more complicated noun phrasal structures can improve performance of the term extractors.

Annotation for under-resourced languages is one of the most challenging problems in natural language processing (NLP). It is difficult to find trained expert annotators in order to ensure a high quality of annotation of the datasets. In this research, the dataset has been annotated by one annotator and we are aware that there can be bias in the dataset. However, the annotations provided here can serve as seed annotations for more sophisticated self-supervised and semi-supervised algorithms which we hope can then establish state-of-the-art benchmarks for under-resourced term extraction. Also, it is important to note that supervised learning algorithms are used to noisy annotate datasets in NLP, however terms are references to domain concepts and we are not aware of any machine learning algorithm that can essentially map concepts; it is one of the longstanding problems in the area of artificial intelligence and therefore the manually annotated dataset presented here better models the domain concepts of education.

Finally, this is an ongoing research and we hope to add more annotators as well as develop better annotation guidelines in order to improve the annotation quality of this dataset in the future. Furthermore, we also intend on adding more documents to the collection so that the dataset can be meaningfully used to train deep learning based architectures for term extraction. From an algorithmic perspective, we plan on the development of novel algorithms which can beat the current state-of-the-art on the task of term extraction for under-resourced languages.

8. Acknowledgement

Author Shubhanker Banerjee was supported by Science Foundation Ireland under Grant Agreement No. 13/RC/2106_P2 at the ADAPT SFI Research Centre at National University Of Ireland Galway. ADAPT, the SFI Research Centre for AI-Driven Digital Content Technology, is funded by Science Foundation Ireland through the SFI Research Centres Programme.

9. Bibliographical References

Astrakhantsev, N. (2018). ATR4S: Toolkit with State-of-the-Art Automatic Terms Recognition Methods in Scala. *Lang. Resour. Eval.*, 52(3):853–872, sep.

Bada, M., Eckert, M., Evans, D., Garcia, K., Shipley, K., Sitnikov, D., Baumgartner, W. A., Cohen, K. B., Verspoor, K., Blake, J. A., and Hunter, L. E. (2012). Concept annotation in the craft corpus. *BMC Bioinformatics*, 13(1):161, Jul.

Bordea, G., Buitelaar, P., and Polajnar, T. (2013). Domain-independent term extraction through domain modelling. In *The 10th international conference on terminology and artificial intelligence (TIA 2013), Paris, France.* 10th International Conference on Terminology and Artificial Intelligence.

Brants, T. (2000). TnT – a statistical part-of-speech tagger. In *Sixth Applied Natural Language Processing Conference*, pages 224–231, Seattle, Washington, USA, April. Association for Computational Linguistics.

Bright, W. (1996). The devanagari script. *The world's writing systems*, pages 384–390.

Cabré, M. T. (1999). *Terminology: Theory, methods, and applications*, volume 1. John Benjamins Publishing.

Church, K. and Gale, W., (1999). *Inverse Document Frequency (IDF): A Measure of Deviations from Poisson*, pages 283–295. Springer Netherlands, Dordrecht.

Cram, D. and Daille, B. (2016). Terminology extraction with term variant detection. In *Proceedings of ACL-2016 system demonstrations*, pages 13–18.

Daille, B. (1994). Study and implementation of combined techniques for automatic extraction of terminology. In *The balancing act: Combining symbolic and statistical approaches to language.*

Evans, D. A. and Lefferts, R. G. (1995). Clarit-trec experiments. *Information processing & management*, 31(3):385–395.

Jacquemin, C. and Bourigault, D. (2005). Term Extraction and Automatic Indexing.

Kachru, Y. (2006). *Hindi*, volume 12. John Benjamins Publishing.

Khurshid, A., Gillman, L., and Tostevin, L. (2000). Weirdness indexing for logical document extrapolation and retrieval. In *Proceedings of the Eighth Text Retrieval Conference (TREC-8).*

Kim, J.-D., Ohta, T., Tateisi, Y., and Tsujii, J. (2003). GENIA corpus—a semantically annotated corpus for bio-textmining. *Bioinformatics*, 19(suppl$_1$) : $i180 - -i182, 07$.

Manning, C., Raghavan, P., and Schütze, H. (2010). Introduction to information retrieval. *Natural Language Engineering*, 16(1):100–103.

McCrae, J. P. and Doyle, A. (2019). Adapting Term Recognition to an Under-Resourced Language: The Case of Irish. In *Proceedings of the Celtic Language Technology Workshop*, pages 48–57.

Meijer, K., Frasincar, F., and Hogenboom, F. (2014). A semantic approach for extracting domain taxonomies from text. *Decision Support Systems*, 62:78–93.

Oliver, A. (2017). A system for terminology extraction and translation equivalent detection in real time: Efficient use of statistical machine translation phrase tables. *Machine Translation*, 31(3):147–161.

Pazienza, M. T., Pennacchiotti, M., and Zanzotto, F. M. (2005). Terminology extraction: An analysis of linguistic and statistical approaches. In Spiros Sirmakessis, editor, *Knowledge Mining*, pages 255–279, Berlin, Heidelberg. Springer Berlin Heidelberg.

Pazienza, M. T. (1998). A domain-specific terminology-extraction system. *Terminology. International Journal of Theoretical and Applied Issues in Specialized Communication*, 5(2):183–201.

Peñas, A., Verdejo, F., and Gonzalo, J. (2001a). Corpus-based terminology extraction applied to information access.

Peñas, A., Verdejo, F., Gonzalo, J., et al. (2001b). Corpus-based terminology extraction applied to information access. In *Proceedings of corpus linguistics*, volume 2001, page 458.

Šajatović, A., Buljan, M., Šnajder, J., and Dalbelo Bašić, B. (2019). Evaluating automatic term extraction methods on individual documents. In *Proceedings of the Joint Workshop on Multiword Expressions and WordNet (MWE-WN 2019)*, pages 149–154, Florence, Italy, August. Association for Computational Linguistics.

Tan, C., Xia, J., Wu, L., and Li, S. Z. (2021). Co-learning: Learning from noisy labels with self-supervision. In *Proceedings of the 29th ACM International Conference on Multimedia*, pages 1405–1413.

Zhang, Z., Gao, J., and Ciravegna, F. (2016). JATE 2.0: Java automatic term extraction with Apache Solr. In *Proceedings of the Tenth International Conference on Language Resources and Evaluation (LREC'16)*, pages 2262–2269, Portorož, Slovenia, May. European Language Resources Association (ELRA).

Zhang, Z., Petrak, J., and Maynard, D. (2018). Adapted textrank for term extraction: A generic method of improving automatic term extraction algorithms. *Procedia Computer Science*, 137:102–108. Proceedings of the 14th International Conference on Semantic Systems 10th – 13th of September 2018 Vienna, Austria.

10. Language Resource References

Zhang, Ziqi and Gao, Jie and Ciravegna, Fabio. (2016). *JATE 2.0: Java Automatic Term Extraction with Apache Solr*. European Language Resources Association (ELRA).

Proceedings of the TERM21 Workshop , pages 26–29
Language Resources and Evaluation Conference (LREC 2022), Marseille, 20-25 June 2022

Terminology extraction using co-occurrence patterns as predictors of semantic relevance

Rogelio Nazar, David Lindemann
Instituto de Literatura y Ciencias del Lenguaje, Pontificia Universidad Católica de Valparaíso
Faculty of Arts, UPV/EHU University of the Basque Country
rogelio.nazar@pucv.cl, david.lindemann@ehu.eus

Abstract

We propose a method for automatic term extraction based on a statistical measure that ranks term candidates according to their semantic relevance to a specialised domain. As a measure of relevance we use term co-occurrence, defined as the repeated instantiation of two terms in the same sentences, in indifferent order and at variable distances. In this way, term candidates are ranked higher if they show a tendency to co-occur with a selected group of other units, as opposed to those showing more uniform distributions. No external resources are needed for the application of the method, but performance improves when provided with a pre-existing term list. We present results of the application of this method to a Spanish-English Linguistics corpus, and the evaluation compares favourably with a standard method based on reference corpora.

Keywords: terminology extraction, co-occurrence patterns, semantic relevance

1. Introduction

In this short paper, we present a methodological proposal for automatic terminology extraction (ATE), which forms part of a larger terminology software project, currently in development, aimed at the automation of different tasks of glossary creation. Here we explain therefore only the task of creating the list of entries for the glossary by means of term extraction from a specialised corpus. With this goal in mind, we experimented with the application of a co-occurring measure, which we used as a means to operationalise a key concept of the ATE problem such as semantic relevance.
Using word co-occurrence as indicator of semantic relevance is something that has been tried in the past for different terminology related applications (Nazar et al., 2007; Wartena et al., 2010). An earlier attempt to use this type of measures in an ATE system was Termout[1] (Nazar, 2016), which proved effective as a method to extract terms from a single document but too computationally expensive to analyse a full corpus, making it impractical in environments like web applications.
On this occasion, we further explore these co-occurrence measures and present a significant improvement. This new method is simple, computationally efficient and scalable: after a classical workflow involving the filtering of single and multi-word units based on syntactic patterns, the central idea is to promote candidates that show a particular profile of co-occurrence, i.e., a tendency to appear with a selected number of other lexical units in the same sentences. This is regardless of the order of appearance of the terms, as well as their relative distance, as in the case of the terms *signifier* and *signified* in the field of Linguistics. We observe that when a candidate has a persistent group of 'friends', it usually is a specialised term, as opposed to those showing more uniform distributions.
The co-occurrence information is obtained from the same specialised corpus, and for this reason, a minimum corpus size is required (ca. 5 million tokens). Apart from a POS-tagger, no external resources are needed. But if a list of terms of the domain is already available, then it can be used to improve performance by identifying its members among the co-occurring words of a given candidate.
We present results of the application of the method to a Spanish-English linguistic corpus, in which evaluation figures compare favourably with a standard method based on reference corpora. More data is available on the project's website[2].

2. Related Work

The field of terminology has always been intrinsically related with that of computational linguistics because of the variety of natural language processing tools and methods that can be applied to at least partially automatise the terminology workflow and the process of dictionary creation (Sager, 1990). ATE, however, was consolidated as a particular field of research after Kageura and Umino's survey (1996), where the authors defined the task of separating the terms from the rest of the vocabulary of a specialised corpus. They also presented the main approaches (i.e., based on statistical or on linguistic knowledge) and explained the procedure for evaluation, which continues to be the standard today.
Different methods have been proposed in the span of several decades, but no consensus has yet been reached concerning which one is preferable, since different methods show a better performance than others, depending on the use case. The lack of a standard evaluation dataset is one of the main difficulties for evalu-

[1] http://www.termout.org

[2] http://www.tecling.com/cgi-bin/termout/ling

ating ATE methods (Astrakhantsev, 2017; Zhang et al., 2017).

Overall, certain tendencies can appreciated in the history of this field. Earlier methods began to explore statistics of term distribution. The work of Spärk-Jones (1972) in Information Retrieval is often credited as a trailblazer in ATE, as she proposed an algorithm to promote term candidates that show concentrated frequency in fewer documents of a corpus. An earlier study by Juilland and Chang-Rodriguez (1964) also deserves mention, as they too were looking at how lexical units are distributed in a corpus in order to separate terms from general vocabulary.

Later models, in the eighties and nineties, involved a greater degree of linguistic sophistication, with the application of morphosyntactic patterns for the correct segmentation of multiword units (Justeson and Katz, 1995). They observed that multiword terms most often occur as certain types of noun phrases (e.g., noun, adjective-noun, noun-preposition-noun).

In parallel, with the rise of Corpus Linguistics in the British lexicographic tradition (Sinclair, 1991), the concept of 'keyness' or 'keywordness' began to develop, according to which lexical units are weighted using large reference corpora of non-specialised discourse. Keywords are defined as those that occur relatively more often in the domain-specific target corpus than would be expected in comparison with a reference corpus that represent general or every-day language. Functions to extract keywords were then offered by classical corpus linguistics software such as Wordsmith Tools (Scott, 1997) or AntConc (Anthony, 2005). Later term extraction systems were also inspired by this approach, such as Termostat (Drouin, 2003), and Sketch Engine (Kilgarriff et al., 2014), and others using similar notions such as term 'weirdness' (Ahmad et al., 1994).

By the turn of the century, surveys show a progressive hybridisation of methodologies, involving both statistical and linguistic data (Cabré et al., 2001). More recently, however, a new tendency seems to be gaining ground, one that takes into account contextual features and distributional semantics. TerMine (Frantzi et al., 2000) is an earlier example of ATE method that uses some form of contextual features. Its 'C-/NC-value' combines statistical measures and distributional information. The common statistical measure is improved in the sense that it adjusts frequency values of single or multiword terms that also occur as part of longer multiword terms (C measure), while information about words that tend to appear next to term candidates is also taken into account (NC measure).

However, it is in more recent approaches where the semantic component is most evident. Some researchers are introducing semantic relatedness of term candidates as a measure in addition to a combination of methods based on statistics (frequencies) and linguistics (lexico-syntactic patterns, distributional information). For instance, 'KeyConceptsRelatedness' (Astrakhantsev, 2014) is the semantic relatedness of candidates to already validated domain terms, where semantic relatedness is computed according to a word embedding model trained on Wikipedia text. Similar work relies on lexico-semantic knowledge represented in semantic networks and ontologies, as shown in the survey by Maynard et al. (2008). In this line, Zhang et al. (2017) propose a generic method for enhancing ATE results, using a small set of validated seed terms to compute the distributional similarity against term candidates.

Our present proposal can be considered similar to this later trend, as it uses co-occurrence to operationalise semantic relevance.

3. Method

As usual in ATE projects, this method begins with the selection of a language and a domain of interest. As we were already embarked in a project to develop a large Spanish-English Linguistics glossary, we decided to test our method with a linguistics corpus. To this end, we used all the articles published in the last 25 years by *Revista Signos*[3], an open-access linguistics journal that accepts papers in both languages. This constitutes a corpus of 602 papers with a total of approximately 6.5 million tokens.

We developed a pipeline to download the papers and convert them from their original HTML format to plain text. As usual in some academic journals, the papers have bilingual titles, abstracts and keywords. They also often mix reference titles mainly in both of these languages. In this paper we set up the ATE task to be applied on monolingual corpora. At a later stage, we will exploit the fact that it is a pseudo-parallel corpus in order to align the extracted terms, but as we said, we leave those details for a future paper. For the present stage, we opted to separate the corpus in both languages and apply the method one language at a time. This separation is done automatically with Linguini[4], a Perl script that detects the main language of every text in a corpus and then deletes any fragments in other languages found inside each text. This is relevant in our use case, since also the text bodies frequently contain e.g. quotes and examples in another language.

As is normal in this type of workflows, the next step in the pre-processing the corpus consists of the application of a POS-tagger. In our case, we used UDPipe (Straka and Straková, 2017) because of the quality of its lemmatisation and POS-tagging. It also offers full syntactic parsing, and some authors have suggested the use of this type of parsers in order to better segment multiword terminology (Judea et al., 2014). However, we opted for a more conservative approach, and ignored the syntactic annotation. Instead, we defined a list of morphosyntactic patterns typical of multiword terminology, such as noun-noun or adjective-noun (e.g., *corpus linguistics, specific language im-*

[3]http://www.revistasignos.cl

[4]http://www.tecling.com/linguini

pairment) or constructions with certain propositions (e.g., in Spanish, *lingüística de corpus*). This is undoubtedly an oversimplification of the problem because morphosyntactic patterns found in multiword terminology can be extremely diverse, and this will have to be addressed in future work.

The previous step results in a first unrefined list of term candidates. Next, the algorithm extracts the contexts of occurrence of each candidate in the specialised corpus. The intuition is that genuine terms of the domain will show a particular profile of co-occurrence, as indicative of how informative they are. This can be seen, for instance, in Figure 1, which depicts this type of analysis for the case of the term *second language acquisition*. In this case, we can see a characteristic shape of the co-occurrence frequency curve, showing that there is a limited number of vocabulary units that appear with a significant frequency in the same sentences. One can notice, among the most frequent co-occurring units, some words and parts of terms and proper names that are semantically related to the candidate (e.g. *learning, feedback, corrective*).

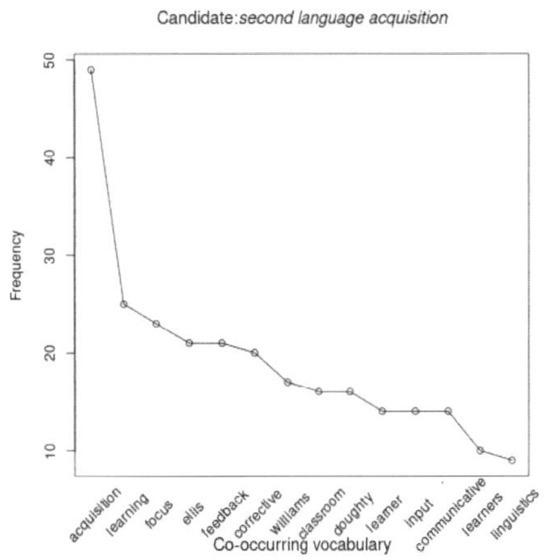

Figure 1: Co-occurrence profile of candidate *second language acquisition* in the corpus.

In order to account for this phenomenon as a predictor of terminology, we developed a co-occurrence measure (1) that will promote a candidate based on its co-occurrence frequency curve.

$$I(x) = \frac{\log_2 \sum_{i=1}^{n} R_{x,i}}{\log_2 |m(x)|} \quad (1)$$

Here, x represents some term candidate; R_x is the set of co-occurring words; $m(x)$ is the set of contexts of occurrence of x and $R_{x,i}$ is the frequency of occurrence of a word in the ith position of the n most frequent words in those contexts. The parameter n is arbitrary, and we set it to 20 in our experiments. Larger values would imply longer processing times.

Another arbitrary parameter would be a threshold k, used by a binary function ATE(x) (2) if one needs to accept or reject each candidate. Alternatively, one can rank all candidates in a list according to (1).

$$ATE(x) = \begin{cases} 1 & I(x) > k \\ 0 & \text{otherwise} \end{cases} \quad (2)$$

As a final note for the explanation of the methodology, we add that the sensitivity of the term detection can be amplified with the use of a pre-existent list of terminological units. If a user can provide a large list of terms as examples (ca. 2000), then the algorithm can calculate the intersection between such list and the vocabulary co-occurring with a candidate. Of course, this is then used to promote a candidate as a relevant term, but it can also be used to narrow down the selection according to the interest of the researcher, e.g. to extract term candidates for the enrichment of a vocabulary of the domain of Lexicography rather than Linguistics.

4. Results and Evaluation

After processing the corpus, the algorithm first obtained a list of approximately 46,000 different noun phrases with term-like morphosyntactic patterns, and then ranked them according to the co-occurrence measure. We only considered as a result the best 4,000 candidates of the list, and we conducted a manual evaluation of the first and the last 500 rank positions. The error rates obtained were 23% and 48%, respectively, with 84% inter-coder agreement.

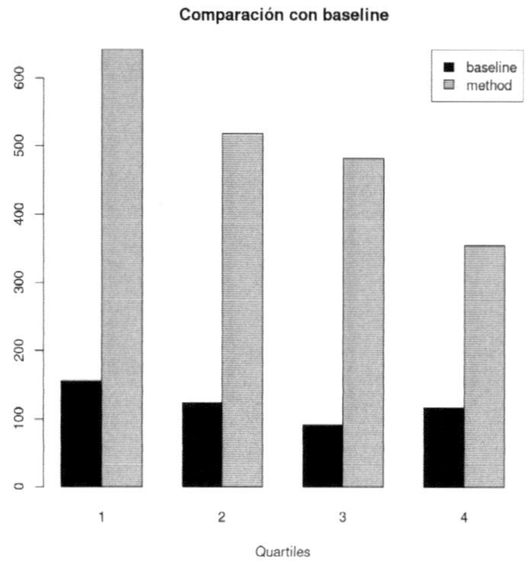

Figure 2: Contrast between method and baseline by the intersection of terms with Gold Standard.

Also, as a baseline we used Sketch Engine's term extraction function (Kilgarriff et al., 2014), as it represents a classical approach based on reference corpora (cf. Section 2). We submitted the same corpus, and again considered only the best 4,000 term candidates. To automatise the comparison, we used as gold-standard a manually curated list of circa 3,500 linguistics terms. Figure 2 shows the comparison with the baseline in the number of matches with the gold standard. The first quartile corresponds to the best 1000 candidates. As can be seen, the matching is significantly higher than the baseline in each quartile, and then it decreases non-randomly, meaning that the ranking is effective.

5. Conclusions

In this paper we proposed an ATE method and described its results on a Spanish-English linguistics corpus. The method is relatively simple, it is computationally efficient and the evaluation shows promising results.

In future work we will be describing subsequent steps to further improve the quality of results. We already mentioned some of these steps, like a better segmentation of multiword terms. But we also discovered other simple strategies which have a significant impact, such as promoting candidates that appear in bibliographic references. We are also working on how to automatise other operations such as filling in fields of a terminological database, such as equivalences in another language, morphological categories, inflected forms, related terms, definitions, and others.

6. Bibliographical References

Ahmad, K., Davies, A., Fulford, H., and Rogers, M. (1994). What is a term?: The semi-automatic extraction of terms from text. In Mary Snell-Hornby, et al., editors, *Benjamins Translation Library*, volume 2, page 267. John Benjamins, Amsterdam.

Anthony, L. (2005). Antconc: Design and development of a freeware corpus analysis toolkit for the technical writing classroom. In *IPCC 2005. Proceedings. International Professional Communication Conference*, pages 729–737.

Astrakhantsev, N. (2014). Automatic term acquisition from domain-specific text collection by using Wikipedia. *Proceedings of the Institute for System Programming of the RAS (Proceedings of ISP RAS)*, 26(4):7–20.

Astrakhantsev, N. (2017). ATR4S: toolkit with state-of-the-art automatic terms recognition methods in Scala. *Language Resources and Evaluation*, 52(3):853–872.

Cabré, M. T., Estopà, R., and Vivaldi, J. (2001). Automatic term detection: A review of current systems. In Didier Bourigault, et al., editors, *Natural Language Processing*, volume 2, pages 53–87.

Drouin, P. (2003). Term extraction using non-technical corpora as a point of leverage. *Terminology*, 9(1):99–115.

Frantzi, K., Ananiadou, S., and Mima, H. (2000). Automatic recognition of multi-word terms:. the c-value/nc-value method. *International Journal on Digital Libraries*, 3(2):115–130.

Judea, A., Schütze, H., and Bruegmann, S. (2014). Unsupervised training set generation for automatic acquisition of technical terminology in patents. In *Proceedings of COLING 2014, the 25th International Conference on Computational Linguistics: Technical Papers*, pages 290–300, Dublin, Ireland, August.

Juilland, A. and Chang-Rodriguez, E. (1964). *Frequency Dictionary of Spanish Words*. De Gruyter.

Justeson, J. S. and Katz, S. M. (1995). Technical terminology: some linguistic properties and an algorithm for identification in text. *Natural Language Engineering*, 1(1):9–27.

Kageura, K. and Umino, B. (1996). Methods of automatic term recognition: A review. *Terminology*, 3(1):259–289.

Kilgarriff, A., Baisa, V., Bušta, J., Jakubíček, M., Kovář, V., Michelfeit, J., Rychlý, P., and Suchomel, V. (2014). The sketch engine: Ten years on. *Lexicography*, 1(1):7–36.

Maynard, D., Li, Y., and Peters, W. (2008). NLP Techniques for Term Extraction and Ontology Population. In Paul Buitelaar et al., editors, *Ontology Learning and Population: Bridging the Gap between Text and Knowledge*, pages 107–127. IOS Press.

Nazar, R., Vivaldi, J., and Wanner, L. (2007). Towards quantitative concept analysis. *Procesamiento del Lenguaje Natural*, 39:139–46.

Nazar, R. (2016). Distributional analysis applied to terminology extraction: First results in the domain of psychiatry in Spanish. *Terminology*, 22(2):141–170.

Sager, J. C. (1990). *A Practical Course in Terminology Processing*. John Benjamins, Amsterdam.

Scott, M. (1997). The right word in the right place: Key word associates in two languages. *AAA: Arbeiten Aus Anglistik Und Amerikanistik*, 22(2):235–248.

Sinclair, J. (1991). *Corpus, Concordance, Collocation*. Oxford University Press.

Spärck Jones, K. (1972). A statistical interpretation of term specificity and its application in retrieval. *Journal of Documentation*, 28:11–21.

Straka, M. and Straková, J. (2017). Tokenizing, POS tagging, lemmatizing and parsing UD 2.0 with UDPipe. In *Proceedings of the CoNLL 2017 Shared Task: Multilingual Parsing from Raw Text to Universal Dependencies*, pages 88–99, Vancouver, Canada.

Wartena, C., Brussee, R., and Slakhorst, W. (2010). Keyword Extraction Using Word Co-occurrence. In *2010 Workshops on Database and Expert Systems Applications*, pages 54–58, August.

Zhang, Z., Gao, J., and Ciravegna, F. (2017). SemRe-Rank: Improving Automatic Term Extraction By Incorporating Semantic Relatedness With Personalised PageRank.

Proceedings of the TERM21 Workshop , pages 30–32
Language Resources and Evaluation Conference (LREC 2022), Marseille, 20-25 June 2022

Evaluating Pre-Trained Language Models for Focused Terminology Extraction from Swedish Medical Records

Oskar Jerdhaf[1], Marina Santini[2], Peter Lundberg[1], Tomas Bjerner[1], Yosef Al-Abasse[1], Arne Jönsson[3], Thomas Vakili[4]
[1]Linköping University Hospital, [2]RISE Research Institutes of Sweden,
[3]Linköping University, [4]Stockholm University

Abstract

In the experiments briefly presented in this abstract, we compare the performance of a generalist Swedish pre-trained language model with a domain-specific Swedish pre-trained model on the downstream task of *focused terminology extraction* of implant terms, which are terms that indicate the presence of implants in the body of patients. The fine-tuning is identical for both models. For the search strategy we rely on KD-Tree that we feed with two different lists of term seeds, one with noise and one without noise. Results shows that the use of a domain-specific pre-trained language model has a positive impact on focused terminology extraction only when using term seeds without noise.

Keywords: terminology extraction, implant terms, generalist BERT, domain-specific BERT

1. Introduction

Intuitively, a domain-specific pre-trained language model should preform better than a generalist pre-trained language model when the downstream task is domain specific. However, this commonsense intuition is not always confirmed by empirical results (Gu et al., 2021; von der Mosel et al., 2021; Zheng et al., 2022). Since the effect of domain-specific pre-trained language models on domain-specific downstream tasks is not fully investigated, in the experiments presented here we further explore this issue. Building domain-specific pre-trained language models is expensive and the implication is that each different domain should then have its own specific pre-trained language model. Obviously, if generalist pre-trained language models perform competitively, considering using generalist models rather than domain-specific models would become a strong option in order to save time and money. We delve more into this issue and we explore the downstream task of focused terminology extraction. Focused terminology extraction indicates the extraction of a relatively small family of specific terms, i.e. terms that represent a specialized semantic field. In this case we focus on the extraction of terms that indicate or suggest the presence of "implants" in electronic medical records (EMRs) written in Swedish.

2. Evaluating Terminology Models

The evaluation of Automatic Terminology Extraction (ATE) models is notoriously difficult. As pointed out during the latest shared task competition at TermEval2020: "Taking into account the unpredictability of many machine learning approaches and the considerable variety between the potential outputs, as demonstrated in this shared task, it is essential for ATE to be evaluated beyond precision, recall, and f1-scores" (Rigouts Terryn et al., 2020). Evaluation is even more difficult in the absence of domains or sub-domains where gold standards are not available. This situation is very common when dealing with the specialized terms that characterize focused terminology extraction. In this case, the terms candidates must be evaluated by domain experts **on the output of focused terminology extraction systems**. With this type of evaluation, that we call *posterior evaluation*, we will only know the number of good candidate terms (yes-terms), bad candidate terms (no-terms) and terms where the annotators feel "unsure", but we remain unaware of the total numbers of good, bad and unsure terms in the whole corpus.

In previous experiments (Jerdhaf et al., 2021)[1], we built a initial gold standard based on the posterior evaluation of a generalist Swedish pre-trained language model. We say "initial" because the gold standard will be incrementally augmented in the way we explain in Section 4. The gold standard for this task has been designed with three categories, namely **yes-terms** (good candidates), **no-terms** (bad candidates) and **u-terms** (unsure and ambiguous terms). This gold standard is the manually evaluated output of a focused terminology extraction model that was fine-tuned on the generalist Swedish KB-BERT model (Malmsten et al., 2020) to discover implant terms unsupervisely. Top ranked candidate implant terms were presented to domain experts (two MRI physicists) for manual evaluation. Results were promising according to our experts. However, we observed that the number of candidate terms that were NOT indicative of implants was quite high. Therefore, we decided to investigate whether a pre-trained domain-specific language model would help in decreasing the number of bad candidates.

[1]The research has been approved by the Swedish Ethical Review Authority (Etikprövningsmyndigheten), authorization number: 2021-00890 to Peter Lundberg.

	Gold Standard	KB-BERT		SweDeClin-BERT	
Term seeds	-	Term seeds w/ noise	Term seeds w/o noise	Term seeds w/ noise	Term seeds w/o noise
YES-terms	1267	648	409	383	575
NO-terms	2930	1503	796	723	73
Discoveries	-	2868	4018	2807	1279
Total	4197	5019	5223	4036	1927

Table 1: Breakdown of terms extracted by the models and the overlap with terms in the gold standard.

3. Data and Datasets

The data used for the downstream task are medical records written in Swedish. We use the medical records of two clinics (cardiology and neurology) that belongs to the LIU-Hospital-EMRs-collection, described in Jerdhaf et al. (2021).

4. Method

The aim of the experiments described below is to compare a focused terminology extraction model fine-tuned on the generalist Swedish pre-trained KB-BERT (Malmsten et al., 2020) with a focused terminology extraction model fine-tuned on the domain-specific (clinical) Swedish pre-trained SweDeClin-BERT (Vakili et al., 2022) on the extraction of implant terms.

Both models have been fine-tuned using the same parameters on the same dataset created from the medical records of two clinics (cardiology and neurology). For the search strategy, we used KDTree (Python, sklearn.neighbors.KDTree) (Pedregosa et al., 2011) with two different lists of term seeds, one with noise (753 terms) and one without noise (1267 implant terms) (see example in Figure 1, right hand-side). Term seeds play a very important role in this type of modelling because they are used to generate random queries. This means that for each term seed, a sentence containing the term was randomly chosen from the dataset and used to find contextually similar sentences. The similarity of contextually similar sentences is based on word embeddings. Essentially, the model will select candidate terms that have a similar role and position as the term seeds of the queries. At this stage of our research the creation of the queries is randomized. This randomization has the advantage of discovering new candidates (that we call *discoveries*) at each run of the model. Discoveries are the terms brought to surface by the randomized queries. The role of discoveries is paramount since it is unthinkable and unfeasible that two or more MRI physicists read millions of medical records and annotate implant terms in one go. In our approach, at each run, the domain experts will be presented new discoveries that, when annotated, will increase the gold standard. An example of how the domain-experts annotate the discoveries is shown in Figure 1, left hand-side. It is a iterative process that will repeat until the majority of discoveries will be in the Yes-term list of the gold standard. It is important to notice that the models will always surface new discoveries because medical records will be added to the current collection over time and because new implant artefacts will be placed on the market and used on patients. What we want to achieve at this point of our research is to identify the model that: 1) maximize the number of good candidate terms already present in the Yes-term list of the gold standard; 2) minimize the number of bad candidate terms already present in the No-term list of the gold standard; 3) return a number of discoveries that when evaluated have the same distribution pattern as described in points 1 and 2, i.e. many good candidates and few bad candidates.

5. Results and Evaluation

According to the results shown in Table 1, the focused terminology extraction model fine-tuned on the domain-specific (clinical) Swedish pre-trained SweDeClin-BERT in combination with term seeds without noise (Column 6) meets the expectations stated in points 1 and 2 of the previous section .

In order to verify the 3rd expectation, we handed over the 1279 discoveries generated by that model to two domain experts. Manual evaluation of the 1279 discoveries meets our expectation as formulated in point 3 because the two domain experts agreed on assessing 750 Yes-terms and they also agreed on rating 91 No-terms. They had discordant ratings on the rest. We observe that the distribution trend of the Yes- and No-terms of the manually evaluated discoveries matches the trend of the Yes- and No-terms found in the gold standard.

6. Discussion

Results shows that the use of a domain-specific pre-trained language model has a positive impact on focused terminology extraction only when using term seeds without noise. This means that a domain-specific pre-trained model has a positive effect under certain conditions.

We are aware that the randomization of the queries as motivated in Section 4 has the downside of conflicting with the principle of experimental replicability. We are currently studying alternative solutions that allow diversification of the results and assure replicability.

7. Conclusion

In this abstract we shortly presented ongoing research on unsupervised focused terminology extraction. Although this is a difficult research area especially for the lack of well-established gold standards and evaluation metrics, results are encouraging. The current gold standard for this task is available for inspection and reuse.

Discoveries	Expert1	Expert2
4074	Y	Y
5076	Y	Y
aai-pacing	Y	Y
ablationsbehandling	U	U
ablationsförsök	U	U
ablationsgruppen	U	U
ablationsingrepp	U	U
ablationsåtgärd	N	U
accessoriusnerven	N	N
acsendensgraft	Y	Y
adl-funktionen	N	N
adp-stimulering	N	U
aggraffer	Y	Y
agiliskateter	Y	Y
agraff	Y	Y
agraffeer	Y	Y
agraffhål	Y	Y
agrafftagning	U	Y
akvedukt	U	Y

```
Term seeds (without noise)
a3dr01
aai-pacemaker
aair-pacemaker
abbot
abbott
activa
acuity
adapta
adapta-dosa
addrl1
agraffer
agrafferna
ai-pacemaker
akveduktstenos
allura
alternativbaksträngsstimulator
amplatz
amplatzer
amplatzer-device
```

Figure 1: Discoveries (left), term seeds without noise (right)

Acknowledgements

This research was funded by **Vinnova** (Sweden's innovation agency), **Grant number**: 2021-0169 and by the **DataLEASH** project.

References

Gu, Y., Tinn, R., Cheng, H., Lucas, M., Usuyama, N., Liu, X., Naumann, T., Gao, J., and Poon, H. (2021). Domain-specific language model pretraining for biomedical natural language processing. *ACM Transactions on Computing for Healthcare (HEALTH)*, 3(1):1–23.

Jerdhaf, O., Santini, M., Lundberg, P., Karlsson, A., and Jönsson, A. (2021). Implant term extraction from swedish medical records–phase 1: Lessons learned. In *Swedish Language Technology Conference and NLP4CALL*, pages 35–49.

Malmsten, M., Börjeson, L., and Haffenden, C. (2020). Playing with words at the national library of Sweden–making a Swedish BERT. *arXiv preprint arXiv:2007.01658*.

Pedregosa, F., Varoquaux, G., Gramfort, A., Michel, V., Thirion, B., Grisel, O., Blondel, M., Prettenhofer, P., Weiss, R., Dubourg, V., et al. (2011). Scikit-learn: Machine learning in python. *the Journal of machine Learning research*, 12:2825–2830.

Rigouts Terryn, A., Hoste, V., Drouin, P., and Lefever, E. (2020). Termeval 2020: Shared task on automatic term extraction using the annotated corpora for term extraction research (acter) dataset. In *6th International Workshop on Computational Terminology (COMPUTERM 2020)*, pages 85–94. European Language Resources Association (ELRA).

Vakili, T., Lamproudis, A., Henriksson, A., and Dalianis, H. (2022). Downstream Task Performance of BERT Models Pre-Trained Using Automatically De-Identified Clinical Data. (Accepted to LREC 2022), June.

von der Mosel, J., Trautsch, A., and Herbold, S. (2021). On the validity of pre-trained transformers for natural language processing in the software engineering domain. *arXiv preprint arXiv:2109.04738*.

Zheng, Z., Lu, X.-Z., Chen, K.-Y., Zhou, Y.-C., and Lin, J.-R. (2022). Pretrained domain-specific language model for general information retrieval tasks in the aec domain. *arXiv preprint arXiv:2203.04729*.

Proceedings of the TERM21 Workshop , pages 33–40
Language Resources and Evaluation Conference (LREC 2022), Marseille, 20-25 June 2022

D-Terminer: Online Demo for Monolingual and Bilingual Automatic Term Extraction

Ayla Rigouts Terryn, Veronique Hoste and Els Lefever
LT3, Language and Translation Technology Team
Department of Translation, Interpreting and Communication – Ghent University
Groot-Brittanniëlaan 45, 9000 Ghent, Belgium
{firstname.lastname}@ugent.be

Abstract

This contribution presents D-Terminer: an open access, online demo for monolingual and multilingual automatic term extraction from parallel corpora. The monolingual term extraction is based on a recurrent neural network, with a supervised methodology that relies on pretrained embeddings. Candidate terms can be tagged in their original context and there is no need for a large corpus, as the methodology will work even for single sentences. With the bilingual term extraction from parallel corpora, potentially equivalent candidate term pairs are extracted from translation memories and manual annotation of the results shows that good equivalents are found for most candidate terms. Accompanying the release of the demo is an updated version of the ACTER Annotated Corpora for Term Extraction Research (version 1.5).

Keywords: automatic term extraction, multilingual term extraction, terminology

1. Introduction

Based on the D-TERMINE (Data-driven Term Extraction Methodologies Investigated) PhD research (Rigouts Terryn, 2021), an online demo, D-Terminer[1], has been developed for automatic term extraction, i.e., the automatic identification of specialised, domain-specific vocabulary in text. The D-Terminer demo supports monolingual term extraction in English, French, Dutch, and German, as well as bilingual automatic term extraction from parallel corpora with pairs of those same languages. The code is open source[2] and the service is freely available, though restrictions apply to the maximum allowed volume of submitted texts. This is an ongoing project with research plans for improvements in many directions, ranging from more advanced term extraction to more customisation and export options. The monolingual methodology has been elaborately described in previous work (Rigouts Terryn et al., 2022), so the current contribution will focus on the methodology and evaluation of the multilingual term extraction.

Accompanying the launch of this demo is the release of an updated version (1.5) of the Annotated Corpora for Term Extraction Research (ACTER) dataset (Rigouts Terryn et al., 2020b), also freely available online under a Creative Commons license (Ayla Rigouts Terryn, Veronique Hoste and Els Lefever, 2022)[3]. Apart from some minor improvements in the annotations themselves (removal of overly long Named Entities and normalisation of accented uppercase "I" character to avoid issues with lowercasing), the main difference is that the annotated terms have now been made available as sequential annotations in the original context, to complement the original format of lists of unique annotations. After a brief overview of the related research, the update of the dataset is discussed. The next section is dedicated to the monolingual term extraction methodology and its implementation into the demo. Next, the methodology and evaluation of the bilingual term extraction are discussed, before concluding with an overview and future research plans.

2. Related Research

Over the past decades, research into monolingual automatic term extraction first evolved from linguistic (e.g., (Justeson and Katz, 1995) and statistical (Sparck Jones, 1972) methodologies to hybrid methodologies. These rule-based hybrid methodologies combine linguistic information like part-of-speech patterns, with statistical metrics used to calculate termhood and unithood (Kageura and Umino, 1996), which measure how related the candidate term (CT) is to the domain, and, in case of candidate multi-word terms, whether the individual components form a cohesive unit. Rule-based hybrid methodologies reached state-of-the-art results for many years, with early work by, a.o., Daille (1994) and Drouin (1997). Variations are still being developed and used more recently as well, e.g. (Kosa et al., 2020; Steingrímsson et al., 2020; Truica and Apostol, 2021). However, (supervised) machine learning methods have become more popular for automatic term extraction, just like for most other areas in natural language processing. Early attempts used algorithms such as AdaBoost (Vivaldi et al., 2001; Patry and Langlais,

[1] D-Terminer demo: `https://lt3.ugent.be/dterminer/`
[2] D-Terminer GitHub repository: `https://github.ugent.be/lt3/D-Terminer/`
[3] ACTER GitHub repository: `https://github.com/AylaRT/ACTER`

2005), RIPPER rule induction (Foo and Merkel, 2010), logistic regression (Nokel, Michael et al., 2012; Fedorenko et al., 2013), and many others. This allowed researchers to combine more information and different kinds of information to detect terms, complementing the traditional linguistic and statistical features, e.g., topic modelling (Bolshakova et al., 2013), consultation of external resources and internet searches (Ramisch et al., 2010), and word embeddings (Wang et al., 2016; Amjadian et al., 2018). The rise of deep learning has seen more neural approaches in recent years, e.g., (Kucza et al., 2018; Shah et al., 2019; Hätty, 2020). The latest trend is the use of language models and sequential methods for automatic term extraction (Gao and Yuan, 2019; Lang et al., 2021), where CTs are detected in their original contexts, usually by classifying each token in text as (part of a) term or not. Most commercial term extraction tools (or tools that include term extraction), e.g., MultiTerm Extract[4] and SketchEngine[5], or online demos by researchers, e.g., TermoStat[6] (Drouin, 2003) and TerMine (Frantzi et al., 2000) rely on rule-based hybrid methodologies.

Multilingual automatic term extraction aims to not only detect CTs, but cross-lingual candidate term pairs. Multilingual term extraction can be performed on parallel corpora, or comparable corpora. The current contribution focuses on the former, i.e., corpora of translations that can be aligned. As discussed by Foo (2012), methodologies can broadly be divided into two groups: "align-extract" and "extract-align", depending on whether monolingual CTs are extracted first, or whether alignment is performed first (so multilingual clues can be considered for the monolingual extraction). As stated by Repar et al. (2019), the former is the more common. Nevertheless, there are indications that multilingual information can help during the monolingual extraction phase. The TExSIS tool for bilingual automatic term extraction from parallel corpora (Macken et al., 2013) starts by extracting word alignments with GIZA++ (Och and Ney, 2003). Next, rule-based chunking is applied (Macken and Daelemans, 2010), after which "a bootstrapping approach is used to extract language-pair specific translation rules" (p. 11). CTs can then be generated based on the aligned phrases, which are further filtered based on statistical (termhood) measures. Whether alignment is performed before or after extraction, Moses phrases tables (Koehn et al., 2007) and GIZA++ (Och and Ney, 2003) remain some of the most popular methodologies for the alignment (Ivanović et al., 2022). The use of language models is generally more common for extraction from comparable corpora.

[4]https://www.trados.com/products/multiterm-desktop/

[5]https://www.sketchengine.eu/

[6]http://termostat.ling.umontreal.ca/

3. ACTER 1.5

For transparency and to encourage similar research, the launch of the demo is accompanied by an updated version of the ACTER dataset. Since the methodology for monolingual term extraction is trained on ACTER, we start with a brief description of the dataset and update. ACTER was first launched in 2020 (Rigouts Terryn et al., 2020a) and is a dataset with comparable corpora[7] in three languages (English, French, Dutch), and four domains (corruption, dressage, heart failure, wind energy). Terms and Named Entities have been manually annotated with four different labels (Specific Terms, Common Terms, Out-of-Domain Terms, and Named Entities). In total, ACTER contains 18,928 unique annotations in corpora of 719,265 tokens. Originally, annotations were only made available as lists of unique (lowercased) annotations (without context). Version 1.5 now includes sequential annotations with IOB labels (Inside, Outside, Beginning) as well. The way these annotations were obtained is well-documented in both the related paper (Rigouts Terryn et al., 2022) and the readme.md file associated with the dataset. This was necessary since the dataset was already starting to be used in sequential methods (Lang et al., 2021), where the lists of annotations were mapped back to the original text. Since the original annotations were made in context, and creating a sequential dataset from these annotations is not always straightforward (due to nested annotations etc.), the annotations have now been made available in this well-documented sequential IO(B) format so researchers can all start from the same dataset and compare results. Additionally, tokenised versions of the annotations as lists are now included as well, since the original annotations do not always coincide with token boundaries. The monolingual models used for D-Terminer are based on this version of ACTER.

4. Monolingual Term extraction

The monolingual term extraction in the D-Terminer demo is a supervised system, trained on ACTER. The method is described in more detail in a previous publication (Rigouts Terryn et al., 2022), which includes a thorough evaluation. Since the exact same methodology is used for the demo, with even more available training data (no held-out test corpus), results will be similar (perhaps even slightly better) than those reported. With the Flair framework (Akbik et al., 2019), a recurrent neural network was trained to tag each sequential token in a domain-specific text as (part of) a term or not, using the biLSTM-CRF architecture and pretrained multilingual BERT embeddings (Devlin et al., 2019). This methodology was shown to perform well, though results remain highly dependent on the domain, language, and relevance of the training data.
For monolingual term extraction with the D-Terminer demo, users are first prompted to upload a domain-

[7]except for one parallel corpus in the domain of corruption

specific corpus of one or more plain text (.txt) files. In contrast to most currently available term extraction tools, which rely on statistical termhood and unithood metrics, the D-Terminer methodology will perform equally well on a small corpus (or even a single sentence), as on a larger corpus. Of course, a larger corpus of domain-specific texts will result in a more comprehensive and representative overview of terms in the domain. This first version of D-Terminer only tokenises the corpus and does not perform additional linguistic preprocessing.

Once the corpus has been uploaded, users are redirected to a new page where they can start the monolingual term extraction. There are three customisable settings pertaining to the training data. The first is to choose between an IOB (Inside-Outside-Beginning) or a binary (IO) tagging scheme. Performance was shown to be similar for both, but can have an impact on the results (e.g., more long terms for IO tagging). The second option concerns the domains on which the system will be trained. Training data will always include all ACTER languages (English, French, Dutch), since the models using multilingual BERT were shown to generalise well across languages. Domain, however, was shown to have a bigger impact on results. To extract terms in a domain that does not resemble any of the domains in ACTER (corruption, dressage, heart failure, and wind energy), it is recommended to use a model trained on the entire dataset. If however, the domain is more closely related, it can be beneficial to use a model trained only on the most similar domain. For instance, the corpus on heart failure is trained on medical abstracts and short papers. These texts contain many terms, and many very specific terms. Therefore, to extract terms in a medical text (even one not related specifically to heart failure), results may be better with the model trained only on the heart failure corpus. More detailed descriptions of the corpora can be found on the demo website. The third and final customisable setting for the monolingual term extraction concerns the types of terms that will be extracted. ACTER contains annotations with four labels: Specific Terms, Common Terms, Out-of-Domain Terms, and Named Entities. Users can select a model that focuses on all, or only on a subset of these labels. Since these three customisable settings are mostly relevant for more advanced users, a standard configuration (IOB labels, all domains, all labels) is offered and recommended.

Results of the monolingual term extraction can be viewed in two ways: either a list of all unique CTs (and their frequencies) in a table, or highlighted CTs in the original texts. These results can also be exported.

5. Bilingual Automatic Term Extraction

5.1. Methodology

For the bilingual automatic term extraction, a bilingual domain-specific corpus can be submitted as a translation memory (one or more .tmx files). First, monolingual term extraction is performed on each language separately, as described above. Users then choose the results of one run of the monolingual extraction in the source language (SL), and one run in the target language (TL), to serve as a starting point for the multilingual extraction. For this multilingual methodology, only CTs that have been extracted in the monolingual phase are considered, so no new instances are added.

Once the appropriate monolingual results for SL and TL have been selected, word alignments are calculated using ASTrED aligned syntactic tree edit distance (Vanroy et al., 2021), which is based on *Awesome Align* (Dou and Neubig, 2021) neural word alignment, that relies on multilingual language models.

Alignment scores per SL and TL CT pair are calculated as 2A + 2B + C, where A = (number of complete matches between SL and TL CT)/(frequency of SL CT), B = average match percentage between SL CT and TL CT, and C = (times SL CT and TL CT occur in same aligned sentence)/(frequency of SL CT). This metric was set experimentally and all alignments with a score of at least 0.5 are currently displayed. The threshold was set low on purpose, to favour recall and provide multiple options which may not always be literal translation, but can still be relevant. As with the monolingual extraction, results can either be viewed in a table as seen in Figure 1, with one or multiple potentially equivalent TL CTs per SL CT, or with the candidate terms in context per document, as in Figure 2, with a parallel scroll for SL and TL texts.

5.2. Evaluation: Annotation

The performance of the multilingual term extraction from parallel corpora was manually evaluated on a bilingual (EN-NL) corpus in the domain of corruption. This corpus is part of the training data for the monolingual term extraction, which means that the results of the monolingual term extraction will be exceptionally good, so the evaluation can focus on the performance of the bilingual alignment. Nevertheless, users should be aware that the multilingual extraction is dependent on the results of the monolingual extractions. The corpus consists mainly of texts from EU institutions, including treaties, reports, and other official communication on the subject of corruption. The English and Dutch parts of the corpus count 52,847 and 54,233 tokens respectively. Monolingual term extraction was performed with the standard settings of the D-Terminer demo (IOB labelling, system trained on all domains and all labels). This resulted in a total of 1129 English CTs and 1367 Dutch CTs. Bilingual extraction was performed as described above, once using English as SL and Dutch as TL, once vice versa. Evaluating the results in both directions was important as this has a considerable impact on results, as will be discussed. Three linguists each annotated 100 EN-NL and 100 NL-EN CT pairs, evaluating both the type of instance and the quality of the alignment. The instances were selected

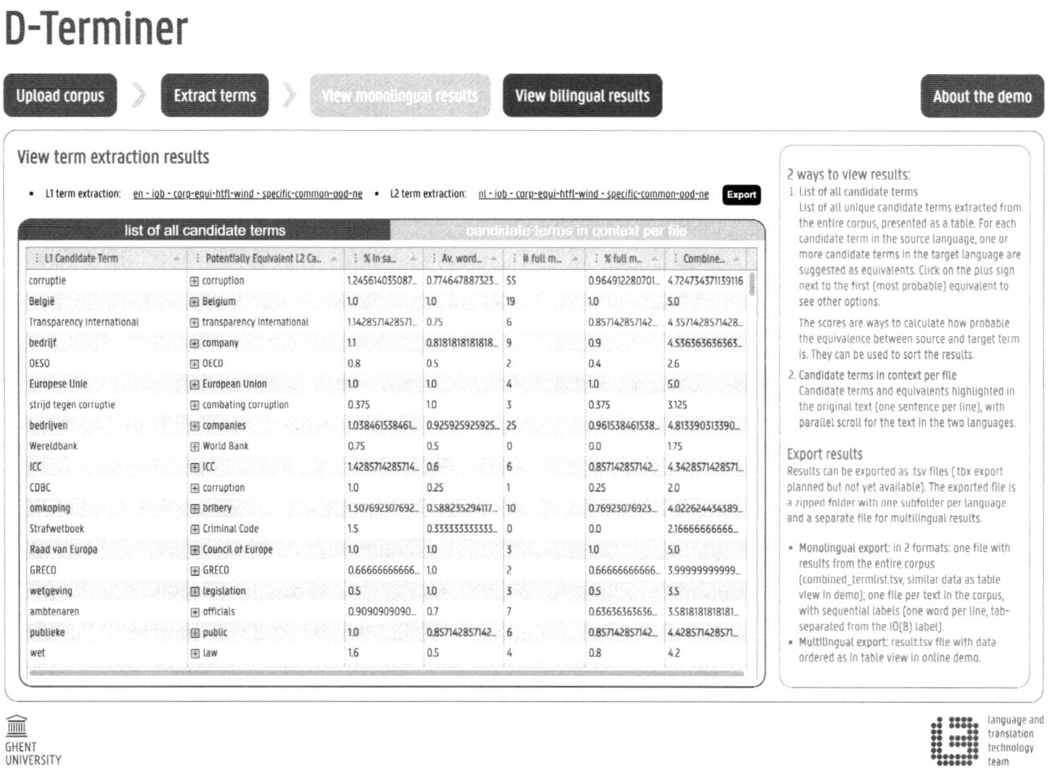

Figure 1: Screenshot of D-Terminer demo, showing multilingual results as list.

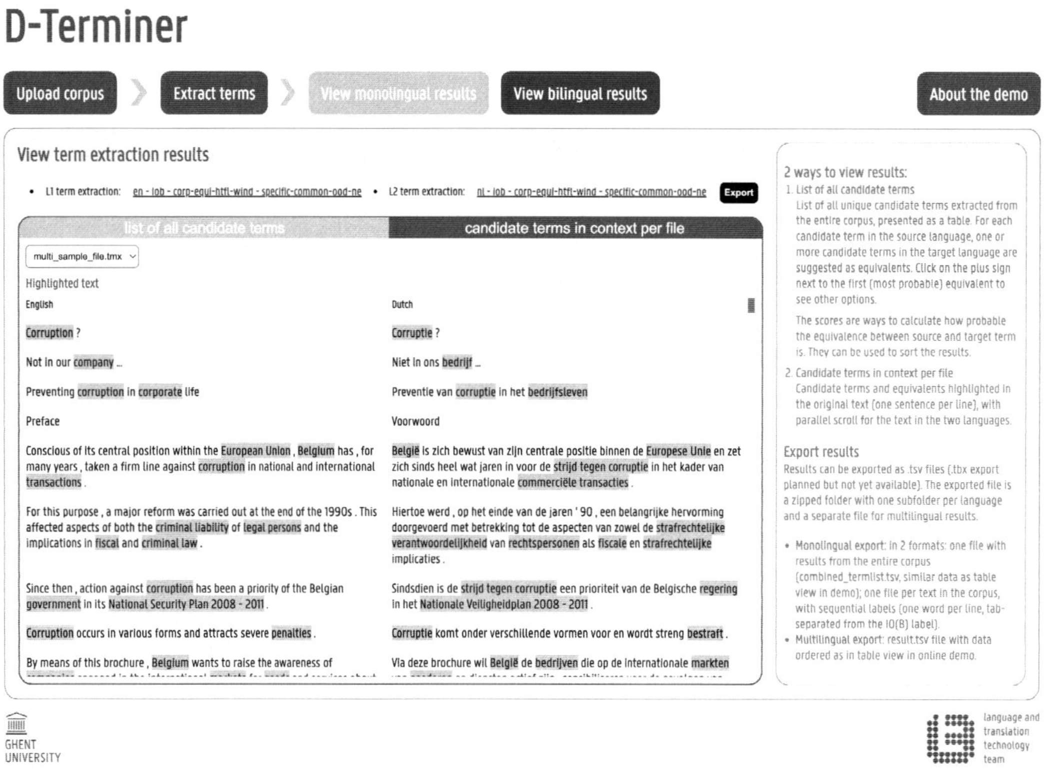

Figure 2: Screenshot of D-Terminer demo, showing multilingual results in context.

by sorting the results by the frequency of the source term, dividing them into 10 sections, and selecting 10 pairs from each section. That way, the evaluation reflects results from different frequency distributions. As there are many CTs that only occur once in the corpus, 41 (EN-NL) and 60 (NL-EN) of the 100 pairs per translation direction were CTs that only occurred once in the entire corpus.

Results were presented to the annotators in a table similar to that used in the online interface (see Figure 1). For each SL CT, annotators had to indicate:

1. Is the **SL CT** a:
   (a) Specific Term (domain- and lexicon-specific),
   (b) Common Term (only domain-specific),
   (c) Named Entity relevant to the domain,
   (d) Named Entity not relevant to the domain, or
   (e) bad candidate (e.g., partial term or Named Entity, clearly neither a term or Named Entity).
2. Is the most highly ranked **TL CT** for the SL CT:
   (a) equivalent,
   (b) equivalent but with a different part-of-speech,
   (c) not equivalent, but useful for a translator, or
   (d) irrelevant

In case the most highly ranked potentially equivalent TL CT was not an exact equivalent (2c or 2d), they also had to indicate whether a correct equivalent was present among the other ranked suggestions and indicate the rank. When the most highly ranked TL CT was found to be a completely irrelevant match (2d) and no exact equivalent was present, they also had to indicate the rank of a potential non-equivalent but relevant TL CT (if present).

Pairwise Cohen's Kappa was used to calculate inter-annotator agreement for annotation tasks 1 (SL CT) and 2 (TL CT). Average agreement (in both translation directions combined) was 0.678 for task 1 and 0.731 for task 2, which are both considered substantial agreement. There were only very small differences between translation directions. Most disagreement on task 1 concerned Specific versus Common Terms (which was expected based on previous experiments (Rigouts Terryn et al., 2020b), especially in this domain). Another recurring issue was differentiating terms from Named Entities, e.g., Named Entities combined with other words/terms (*EU Anti-corruption Reports*) and relevant institutions (*Court of Auditors*). For the annotations of the TL CT, most disagreement was found between the *not equivalent but relevant* and *irrelevant* categories, especially in cases where the suggested equivalent was part of a correct equivalent, e.g., *legal - rechtspersoon [EN: legal person]*, and *anticorruptiestrategie [EN: anti-corruption strategy] - anticorruption*. This is related to the different compounding strategies in Dutch and English (discussed in the next section).

5.3. Evaluation: Results and Discussion

In Table 1, the results of the annotations for both SL and TL CTs can be seen per translation direction and per annotator. The first observation is that the results of the monolingual extraction are very good in both languages. On average, only 5 out of 200 extracted and evaluated CTs were found to be bad candidates. This was expected since the corpus was included in the training data for the monolingual extraction, allowing us to focus on the cross-lingual alignments, i.e., the results of the TL CT evaluation.

The multilingual results are good as well, but with a bigger difference between the languages. For most SL CTs, the most highly ranked potentially equivalent TL CT was evaluated as an actual valid equivalent of the SL CT. For the remainder of this contribution, the evaluation of the suggested equivalent (TL CT) will be based on majority voting, i.e., correct if at least 2 annotators label the TL CT as 2a or 2b. The most highly ranked TL CT was evaluated as a correct equivalent 75.5% of the time. For another 12.5%, an exact equivalent was found among the more lowly ranked suggestions, leaving only 12% of all evaluated CTs without any exact equivalents among the suggested TL CTs. For those 12%, a relevant suggestion was found in most cases and only in 4.5% of the evaluated cases, no relevant suggestion was made at all, including Specific Terms, Common Terms, and Named Entities. Looking at these instances in more detail, a number of explanations can be found. The first and most common cause for a lack of good equivalents in the TL is that the appropriate equivalent was not always extracted during the monolingual extraction phase. For instance, the Dutch CTs *standaardclausules* and *clausules* [EN: *standard clauses* and *clauses*] could not be matched to their English equivalents, because the English forms were not extracted as CTs. This regularly happens because of the different compounding rules in English in Dutch. In Dutch, there are many single-word compounds, of which the equivalent would be written in two words in English. In some cases, this means the Dutch compound is considered a term or Named Entity, while only a part of the English equivalent would be considered as such. For instance, the Dutch *WTO-partners* seems to be a relevant term or Named Entity, but is written as 2 separate words in English (*WTO partners*), where it is logical to extract only *WTO*, so the Dutch CT cannot be matched to the complete equivalent in English, because the latter has not been extracted. Another recurring issue is when the correct equivalent is not present in the source segments, either due to bad alignment, or rephrasing in the translations.

Of the 9 instances for which no relevant or useful equivalents were found at all, only 2 occur more than once. The first is a bad CT: *BUILDING*, which is part of an all-caps title and falsely identified as a CT. It occurs 7 times in total (mostly lowercased in general contexts). The second CT that occurs more than once

		EN-NL				NL-EN			
		Ann1	**Ann2**	**Ann3**	**Av.**	**Ann1**	**Ann2**	**Ann3**	**Av.**
SL CT	a. Specific Term	46	42	59	**49**	50	48	62	**53**
	b. Common Term	22	24	16	**21**	21	25	14	**20**
	c. Relevant Named Entity	16	12	10	**13**	19	15	15	**16**
	d. Irrelevant Named Entity	13	15	14	**14**	9	10	9	**9**
	e. Bad Candidate	3	7	1	**4**	1	2	0	**1**
TL CT	a. Equivalent	79	78	81	**79**	63	61	63	**62**
	b. Equivalent, different POS	3	2	3	**3**	2	1	2	**2**
	c. Not equivalent, relevant	9	9	5	**8**	15	14	3	**11**
	d. Irrelevant, with ranked equiv.	4	4	5	**4**	9	11	16	**12**
	e. Irrelevant, no ranked equiv.	5	7	6	**6**	11	13	16	**13**

Table 1: Annotations of SL CT and most highly ranked option for potentially equivalent TL CT, per language direction and per annotator, including average over all annotators. Since there are 100 instances per experiment, the numbers can be interpreted as percentages.

and for which no good equivalent was found is *instrumentalities*, which occurs twice. The correct equivalent (*hulpmiddelen*) is a more common word in Dutch and was not found by the monolingual extraction. Overall, the system performs slightly better on CTs that occur more than once. For CTs that occur twice or more, the most highly ranked potentially equivalent TL CT is correct 88% of the time, versus 69% of the time for SL CTs that occur only once. The label of the SL CT has a small impact (exact impact depends on annotator), but performance is consistently best for Named Entities (83%) and worst for Specific Terms (71%), with Common Terms in between (80%) (numbers based on SL CT annotations of Annotator 2).
There are a few instances of equivalents with different parts-of-speech, e.g., *investing - investering [EN: investment]*, though this is relatively rare (about 5 out of 200 annotated instances). On average, 8 to 11 percent was annotated as non-equivalent but relevant. Most of these concern pairs where one of the CTs is an equivalent of part of the other CT, e.g., *Court of Auditors - Europese Rekenkamer [EN: European Court of Auditors]*, and *basisdelicten [EN: predicate offences] - offences*. Sometimes, they also concern bad SL CTs, e.g., one which has part of a footnote attached due to bad tokenisation: *criminal justice[54 - strafrecht [EN: criminal justice]*.

6. Conclusion and Future Work

The current contribution describes D-Terminer, an online demo for monolingual and bilingual automatic term extraction. The monolingual extraction is a supervised system trained on annotated data that uses a recurrent neural network to detect terms in context. Users can also upload a parallel corpus in the form of a translation memory to perform bilingual term extraction, and automatically detect potentially equivalent term pairs. Future work on this demo will include more export options (e.g., export as TBX, export of only validated CTs), more advanced monolingual term extraction (combining language model with features), and more linguistic preprocessing (to, e.g., be able to group CTs by lemma). In addition to the online demo, version 1.5 of the ACTER dataset was released, which makes sequential annotations available to users to support research on supervised neural methodologies for term extraction.

7. Acknowledgements

We thank Michaël Lumingu for his help in creating the online D-Terminer demo.

8. Bibliographical References

Akbik, A., Bergmann, T., Blythe, D., Rasul, K., Schweter, S., and Vollgraf, R. (2019). FLAIR: An Easy-to-Use Framework for State-of-the-Art NLP. In *Proceedings of the 2019 Conference of the North American Chapter of the Association for Computational Linguistics: Demonstrations*, pages 54–59, Minneapolis, USA. Association for Computational Linguistics.

Amjadian, E., Inkpen, D. Z., Paribakht, T. S., and Faez, F. (2018). Distributed Specificity for Automatic Terminology Extraction. *Terminology. International Journal of Theoretical and Applied Issues in Specialized Communication*, 24(1):23–40.

Bolshakova, E., Loukachevitch, N., and Nokel, M. (2013). Topic Models Can Improve Domain Term Extraction. In David Hutchison, et al., editors, *Advances in Information Retrieval*, volume 7814, pages 684–687. Springer Berlin Heidelberg, Berlin, Heidelberg.

Daille, B. (1994). *Approche Mixte Pour l'Extraction de Terminologie : Statistique Lexicale et Filtres Linguistiques*. PhD thesis in applied sciences, Université Paris Diderot - Paris 7, Paris, France.

Devlin, J., Chang, M.-W., Lee, K., and Toutanova, K. (2019). BERT: Pre-training of Deep Bidirectional Transformers for Language Understanding. *arXiv:1810.04805 [cs]*.

Dou, Z.-Y. and Neubig, G. (2021). Word alignment by fine-tuning embeddings on parallel corpora. In *Conference of the European Chapter of the Association for Computational Linguistics (EACL)*.

Drouin, P. (1997). Une Méthodologie d'Identification Automatique des Syntagmes Terminologiques : l'Apport de la Description du Non-terme. *Meta: Journal des traducteurs*, 42(1):45–54.

Drouin, P. (2003). Term Extraction Using Non-Technical Corpora as a Point of Leverage. *Terminology. International Journal of Theoretical and Applied Issues in Specialized Communication*, 9(1):99–115.

Fedorenko, D., Astrakhantsev, N., and Turdakov, D. (2013). Automatic Recognition of Domain-specific Terms: An Experimental Evaluation. In *Proceedings of the Ninth Spring Researcher's Colloquium on Database and Information Systems*, volume 26, pages 15–23, Kazan, Russia.

Foo, J. and Merkel, M. (2010). Using Machine Learning to Perform Automatic Term Recognition. In *Proceedings of the LREC 2010 Workshop on Methods for Automatic Acquisition of Language Resources and Their Evaluation Methods*, pages 49–54, Valetta, Malta. European Language Resources Association.

Foo, J. (2012). *Computational Terminology: Exploring Bilingual and Monolingual Term Extraction*. Thesis, Linköping Institute of Technology at Linköping University, Linköping.

Frantzi, K., Ananiadou, S., and Mima, H. (2000). Automatic Recognition of Multi-Word Terms: The C-value/NC-value Method. *International Journal of Digital Libraries*, 3(2):117–132.

Gao, Y. and Yuan, Y. (2019). Feature-less End-to-end Nested Term extraction. In Jie Tang, et al., editors, *Proceedings of Natural Language Processing and Chinese Computing*, pages 607–616, Cham. Springer International Publishing.

Hätty, A. (2020). *Automatic Term Extraction for Conventional and Extended Term Definitions Across Domains*. Ph.D. thesis, Universitat Stuttgart, Stuttgart.

Ivanović, T., Stanković, R., Todorović, B. Š., and Krstev, C. (2022). Corpus-based Bilingual Terminology Extraction in the Power Engineering Domain. *Terminology. International Journal of Theoretical and Applied Issues in Specialized Communication*, April.

Justeson, J. and Katz, S. (1995). Technical Terminology: Some Linguistic Properties and an Algorithm for Identification in Text. *Natural Language Engineering*, 1(1):9–27.

Kageura, K. and Umino, B. (1996). Methods of Automatic Term Recognition. *Terminology. International Journal of Theoretical and Applied Issues in Specialized Communication*, 3(2):259–289.

Koehn, P., Zens, R., Dyer, C., Bojar, O., Constantin, A., Herbst, E., Hoang, H., Birch, A., Callison-Burch, C., Federico, M., Bertoldi, N., Cowan, B., Shen, W., and Moran, C. (2007). Moses: Open Source Toolkit for Statistical Machine Translation. In *Proceedings of the 45th Annual Meeting of the ACL on Interactive Poster and Demonstration Sessions - ACL '07*, pages 177–180, Prague, Czech Republic. Association for Computational Linguistics.

Kosa, V., Chaves-Fraga, D., Dobrovolskyi, H., and Ermolayev, V. (2020). Optimized Term Extraction Method Based on Computing Merged Partial C-Values. In *Information and Communication Technologies in Education, Research, and Industrial Applications. ICTERI 2019*, volume 1175 of *Communications in Computer and Information Science*, pages 24–49. Springer International Publishing, Cham.

Kucza, M., Niehues, J., Zenkel, T., Waibel, A., and Stüker, S. (2018). Term Extraction via Neural Sequence Labeling a Comparative Evaluation of Strategies Using Recurrent Neural Networks. In *Proceedings of Interspeech 2018, the 19th Annual Conference of the International Speech Communication Association*, pages 2072–2076, Hyderabad, India, September. International Speech Communication Association.

Lang, C., Wachowiak, L., Heinisch, B., and Gromann, D. (2021). Transforming Term Extraction: Transformer-Based Approaches to Multilingual Term Extraction Across Domains. In *Findings of the Association for Computational Linguistics: ACL-IJCNLP 2021*, pages 3607–3620, Online. Association for Computational Linguistics.

Macken, L. and Daelemans, W. (2010). A Chunk-Driven Bootstrapping Approach to Extracting Translation Patterns. In David Hutchison, et al., editors, *Computational Linguistics and Intelligent Text Processing*, volume 6008 of *Lecture Notes in Computer Science*, pages 394–405. Springer Berlin Heidelberg, Berlin, Heidelberg.

Macken, L., Lefever, E., and Hoste, V. (2013). TExSIS: Bilingual Terminology Extraction from Parallel Corpora Using Chunk-based Alignment. *Terminology. International Journal of Theoretical and Applied Issues in Specialized Communication*, 19(1):1–30.

Nokel, Michael, Bolshakova, E.i., and Loukachevitch, Natalia. (2012). Combining Multiple Features for Single-word Term Extraction. In *Proceedings of Dialog 2012*, pages 490–501.

Och, F. J. and Ney, H. (2003). A Systematic Comparison of Various Statistical Alignment Models. *Computational Linguistics*, 29(1):19–51.

Patry, A. and Langlais, P. (2005). Corpus-Based Terminology Extraction. In *Terminology and Content Development - Proceedings of the 7th International Conference on Terminology and Knowledge Engineering*, pages 313–321, Copenhagen, Denmark.

Ramisch, C., Villavicencio, A., and Boitet, C. (2010). Mwetoolkit: A Framework for Multiword Expression Identification. In *Proceedings of the Seventh International Conference on Language Resources and Evaluation (LREC'10)*, pages 662–669, Valetta, Malta. European Language Resources Association.

Repar, A., Podpečan, V., Vavpetič, A., Lavrač, N., and Pollak, S. (2019). TermEnsembler: An Ensemble Learning Approach to Bilingual Term Extraction and Alignment. *Terminology. International Journal of Theoretical and Applied Issues in Specialized Communication*, 25(1):93–120.

Rigouts Terryn, A., Hoste, V., Drouin, P., and Lefever, E. (2020a). TermEval 2020: Shared Task on Automatic Term Extraction Using the Annotated Corpora for Term Extraction Research (ACTER) Dataset. In Béatrice Daille, et al., editors, *Proceedings of the LREC 2020 6th International Workshop on Computational Terminology (COMPUTERM 2020)*, pages 85–94, Marseille, France. European Language Resources Association.

Rigouts Terryn, A., Hoste, V., and Lefever, E. (2020b). In No Uncertain Terms: A Dataset for Monolingual and Multilingual Automatic Term Extraction from Comparable Corpora. *Language Resources and Evaluation*, 54(2):385–418.

Rigouts Terryn, A., Hoste, V., and Lefever, E. (2022). Tagging Terms in Text: A Supervised Sequential Labelling Approach to Automatic Term Extraction. *Terminology. International Journal of Theoretical and Applied Issues in Specialized Communication*, 28(1).

Rigouts Terryn, A. (2021). *D-TERMINE: Data-driven Term Extraction Methodologies Investigated*. Doctoral thesis, Ghent University, Ghent, Belgium.

Shah, S., Sarath, S., and Shreedhar, R. (2019). Similarity Driven Unsupervised Learning for Materials Science Terminology Extraction. *Computación y Sistemas*, 23(3):1005–1013.

Sparck Jones, K. (1972). A Statistical Interpretation of Term Specificity and its Application in Retrieval. *Journal of documentation*, 28(1):11–21.

Steingrímsson, S., orbergsdóttir, Á., Danielsson, H., and Ornolfsson, G. T. (2020). TermPortal: A Workbench for Automatic Term Extraction from Icelandic Texts. In *Proceedings of the 6th International Workshop on Computational Terminology (COMPUTERM 2020)*, pages 8–16, Marseille, France. European Association for Machine Translation.

Truica, C.-O. and Apostol, E.-S. (2021). TLATR: Automatic Topic Labeling Using Automatic (Domain-Specific) Term Recognition. *IEEE Access*, 9:76624–76641.

Vanroy, B., De Clercq, O., Tezcan, A., Daems, J., and Macken, L. (2021). Metrics of Syntactic Equivalence to Assess Translation Difficulty. In Michael Carl, editor, *Explorations in Empirical Translation Process Research*, volume 3, pages 259–294. Springer International Publishing, Cham.

Vivaldi, J., Màrquez, L., and Rodríguez, H. (2001). Improving Term Extraction by System Combination Using Boosting. In Luc Raedt et al., editors, *Proceedings of the 12th European Conference on Machine Learning (ECML 2001)*, volume 2167, pages 515–526, Berlin, Heidelberg. Springer Berlin Heidelberg.

Wang, R., Liu, W., and McDonald, C. (2016). Featureless Domain-Specific Term Extraction with Minimal Labelled Data. In *Proceedings of Australasian Language Technology Association Workshop*, pages 103–112, Melbourne, Australia.

9. Language Resource References

Ayla Rigouts Terryn, Veronique Hoste and Els Lefever. (2022). *ACTER Annotated Corpora for Term Extraction Research, version 1.5*. distributed via CLARIN: http://hdl.handle.net/20.500.12124/38.

Author Index